GLOBAL
GENDER
INTELLIGENCE

The Science of Success
in Business, Love,
and Life

GLOBAL GENDER INTELLIGENCE

FEATURING
John Gray Ph.D.
Author of the phenomenal #1 bestseller
Men Are from Mars, Women Are from Venus

AND HIS CERTIFIED
MARS VENUS **COACHES**

First published in 2025 by Dean Publishing
PO Box 119
Mt. Macedon, Victoria, 3441
Australia
deanpublishing.com

Copyright © Mars Venus Coaching
5940 S Rainbow Blvd
Las Vegas, NV 89118
marsvenuscoaching.com

All rights reserved. No part of this publication may be reproduced, stored in a retrieval system or transmitted in any way or by any means, electronic, mechanical, photocopying, recording or otherwise, without the prior written permission of the author and publisher.

Cataloguing-in-Publication Data
National Library of Australia
Title: Global Gender Intelligence
ISBN: 978-0-648995-78-4
Category: Relationships/personal development

The views and opinions expressed in this book are those of the author and do not necessarily reflect the official policy or position of any other agency, publisher, organization, employer or company. Assumptions made in the analysis are not reflective of the position of any entity other than the author(s) – and, these views are always subject to change, revision, and rethinking at any time.
The author, publisher or organizations are not to be held responsible for misuse, reuse, recycled and cited and/or uncited copies of content within this book by others.
This book is not intended as a substitute for the medical advice of physicians or psychologists. The reader should regularly consult a professional in matters relating to his/her health and or relationship issues that require professional help. The ideas within this book are only the opinion of the authors and are not intended to replace any medical advice or relationship advice. Always consult a professional for your health and wellbeing.

CONTRIBUTORS

DR. JOHN GRAY

RICH BERNSTEIN

SUSAN DEAN

DR. ABDULRAHMAN AL-DAYEL

BEATRICE WÖLNER-HANSSEN & STEFAN BURTH

ERIC LANTHIER

JANEZ ZAVAŠNIK

KAWAL ARORA

MAIBA MARINO

MALCOLM BRETT

MARISA YNEZ

MICHAEL DEAN

MONIQUE SARUP

PETRA FÜRST

PETRA ZAVAŠNIK

SAMUEL SINGER

SOPHIA KONSTANTINOVNA

STACY HAVLICEK

CONTENTS

DR. JOHN GRAY – 1
THE SCIENCE OF SUCCESS IN BUSINESS, LOVE, AND LIFE

SUSAN DEAN – 7
A JOURNEY OF COACHING, CONNECTION, AND CONTRIBUTION

DR. ABDULRAHMAN AL-DAYEL – 19
LIFE IS A LESSON: EMBRACE CONTINUOUS LEARNING

SOPHIA KONSTANTINOVNA – 29
FROM FOOTWORK TO SOULWORK:
RECLAIM YOUR RHYTHM IN LIFE, LOVE, AND LEADERSHIP

JANEZ ZAVAŠNIK – 43
ENGINEERING BETTER LIVES

MAIBA MARINO – 59
GENDER INTELLIGENCE IS THE FUTURE

DR. MICHAEL-RAY DEAN – 71
A LIFE BUILT ON GENDER INTELLIGENCE

BEATRICE WÖLNER-HANSSEN & STEFAN BURTH – 83
TRUE TRANSFORMATION COMES FROM WITHIN

MARISA YNEZ – 95
THE SUPERPOWER OF GENDER INTELLIGENCE

KAWAL ARORA 113
MARS VENUS IN INDIA: LOVE BEYOND EXPECTATIONS

PETRA ZAVAŠNIK – 129
EVERYTHING WE NEED IS ALREADY WITHIN US

SAMUEL SINGER – 143
THE WORLD IS BUILT ON RELATIONSHIPS

MONIQUE SARUP – 155
THE HEART OF TEAMWORK:
LOVE, COMMUNICATION, AND GENDER INTELLIGENCE

MALCOLM BRETT – 169
LIFE AND LOVE ARE AN ADVENTURE

STACY HAVLICEK – 187
EMBRACE YOUR AUTHENTIC ENERGY

ERIC LANTHIER – 199
TRUTH LIES BENEATH THE SURFACE

PETRA FÜRST – 215
WHEN SCIENCE MEETS SOUL

RICH BERNSTEIN – 231
GENDER INTELLIGENC: THE KEY TO BUSINESS SUCCESS

ENDNOTES – 244

UNLOCK EXCLUSIVE BONUS CONTENT!

Dr. John Gray and his certified coaches have created powerful resources to enhance your understanding of gender intelligence and the wider Mars Venus philosophy.

Inside your free bonus pack, you'll get:
- Audio downloads
- Printable worksheets
- Practical tools and resources—and more!

Visit **marsvenuscoaching.com/bookbonus** to access your bonuses now.

INTRODUCTION

The Science of Success in Business, Love, and Life

DR. JOHN GRAY

John Gray is the author of the most well-known and trusted relationship book of all time, *Men Are from Mars, Women Are from Venus*. USA Today listed his book as one of the top 10 most influential books of the last quarter-century. In hardcover, it was the number one bestselling book of the 1990s. John's books have been translated into approximately 45 languages in more than 100 countries and continue to be bestsellers.

John helps men and women better understand and respect their differences in both personal and professional relationships.

His approach combines specific communication techniques with healthy nutritional choices that create the brain and body chemistry for lasting health, happiness, and romance.

His many books, blogs, and free online workshops at MarsVenusCoaching.com provide practical insights to improve relationships at all stages of life and love. An advocate of health and optimal brain function, he also provides natural solutions for overcoming depression, anxiety, and stress to support increased energy, libido, hormonal balance, and better sleep.

John has appeared repeatedly on *The Oprah Winfrey Show*, as well as on *The Dr. Oz Show, TODAY, CBS This Morning, Good Morning America*, and many others. He has been profiled in *Time, Forbes, USA Today*, and *People*. He was also the subject of a three-hour special hosted by Barbara Walters.

Dr. John Gray lives in Northern California where he happily shared his life with his beautiful wife, Bonnie, until her passing in 2018. They have three grown daughters and four grandchildren. John is an avid follower of his own health and relationship advice.

In the late 70s, the movement—as far as counseling goes—was to attempt to recognize men and women as the same, completely equal in every way, including the way they think, process emotions, handle stress, and work in relationships. As a counselor and coach, I saw that this model simply wasn't working. Men were trying to think like women. Women were trying to think like men. At the same time, they were struggling to truly understand each other. Because naturally, biologically, *scientifically*, men and women think differently. People think differently. If we truly were all the same, we'd all be pursuing the same goals, the same careers, the same dreams. But individually, we're different. Across genders, we're different again.

To me, equality doesn't mean sameness. It means respecting our differences. Ironically, in our modern era of diversity and inclusion, we often don't respect the differences between men and women, even though many of those differences are biological and hardwired into our brains.

To create positive social change, we must build awareness around our innate differences, developing our gender intelligence to improve our relationships in all areas of life. Men and women don't need "fixing" for acting like themselves. They simply need to be understood.

If more people knew and understood the differences between genders, we could fix so many problems in our society. I created my Mars Venus Coaching program and wrote my 20-plus books, including *Global Gender Intelligence,* with one goal in mind: to help others understand and apply the concepts

I've refined over decades of research and practical coaching experience to improve their relationships, ultimately making the world a better place—for everyone.

When I was developing the Mars Venus philosophy, I never set out to create a coaching program. However, after publishing *Men Are from Mars, Women Are from Venus*, I received countless letters—people even stopped me on the street—explaining how the methods and insights described in the book had transformed their relationships and, in turn, their lives. Many wanted to know how they could help spread the message within their families, workplaces, and communities. What an amazing response from readers! And it got me thinking …

How can we equip more people with the tools to improve their relationships? How can we help more people take a gender-intelligent approach to love, life, and business? How can we make a bigger positive impact in the world? As I've said many times, "I'm only one guy with a great message. I can only do so much myself." As I spoke with more of my readers, I realized many of them were counselors and coaches. *Light-bulb moment.* Alone, I could only run so many workshops and seminars. But if I trained other coaches in my methodologies, they could teach the Mars Venus philosophy locally and in other languages, helping their clients implement it in their own lives to improve their relationships. Finally, I no longer needed to spread the message alone.

With too high divorce rates and frequent instances of workplace conflict and misunderstanding, now more than ever, we must apply gender intelligence to all areas of life—at home *and* in the workplace.[1] How many relationships could be saved with a deep understanding of the opposite gender? How many workplace conflicts could be swiftly resolved or completely avoided with that same understanding? The health and happiness of our society depend on the strength of our relationships. We must spread the message, ensuring every human is equipped with the tools to successfully navigate their relationships and their lives—and our team of certified Mars Venus coaches have risen to the occasion.

In *Global Gender Intelligence: The Science of Success in Business, Love, and Life*—which I've co-authored with 17 of my amazing Mars Venus Coaches—the power and purpose of gender intelligence is made clear. Within these pages, you'll find stories of triumph over adversity, practical tools you can immediately apply to your own life and relationships, and scientific insights that explain exactly why developing gender intelligence is so impactful. What better group of experts to introduce you to, or enhance your knowledge of, the Mars Venus philosophy than those who live and share it every day—our ever-inspiring Mars Venus coaches?

As coaches, our job is to bring out the best in our clients, showing them that happiness and success are achievable and, importantly, *sustainable*. *Global Gender Intelligence* brings our Mars Venus methodologies into the modern era. While the social and political landscapes have changed, one fact remains the same: men and women think differently, act differently, and therefore must be coached differently.

We've trained and certified over 750 Mars Venus coaches in 43 countries around the world, and our message has never been stronger or more widespread—more *global*. Together, we're on a mission to transform lives—one relationship, one breakthrough, one meaningful change at a time. We're not just teaching methods and tools. We're building a movement to create stronger relationships, thriving individuals, and a better world, and our Mars Venus coaches are at the forefront of that movement.

At a time when society and gender dynamics are rapidly shifting, understanding and applying gender intelligence has never been more critical to success in business, love, and life.

A JOURNEY OF COACHING, CONNECTION, AND CONTRIBUTION

SUSAN DEAN

Susan Dean has always been passionate about helping people unlock their full potential. She began her career as a youth worker, supporting teenagers through some of life's toughest challenges. That calling to make a difference soon expanded to adults, and she went on to train with global leaders like Dr. John Gray, becoming a sought-after life, business, and relationship coach and the world's first female Mars Venus coach.

As her coaching and speaking work grew into a thriving business, Susan discovered another way to help people share their wisdom and transform lives—through books. In 2010, she founded Dean Publishing, a boutique, family-run publishing house dedicated to amplifying voices that matter. What started as one woman's vision has grown into a trusted name among entrepreneurs, speakers, coaches, and experts across health, wealth, mindset, spirituality, and business.

At her core, Susan is more than a publisher. She's a wife to her childhood sweetheart Michael, mom to Chloe and Monique (who now help run the business), and proud grandmother of three. Family is woven into every part of her work, making Dean Publishing not just a company, but a legacy.

Susan's greatest joy is helping people turn their knowledge, experience, and stories into books that change lives—starting with their own.

A PRACTICAL APPROACH TO BUSINESS, LOVE, AND LIFE

When I first trained with Dr. John Gray back in 2003, becoming his very first female coach, I could never have imagined I would one day be co-authoring and publishing books with him. At that time, I was simply fascinated by the way his work transformed relationships and created understanding between men and women. It was practical, it was real, and it worked.

What I've always loved about John is, even with his incredible global success, he has remained grounded, approachable, and generous with his wisdom. In fact, one of my favorite memories was interviewing him in Bali during a Mars Venus conference in 2024. What he shared in that conversation was not only inspiring, but also such a powerful reminder of what it really takes to be successful, not just as an author, but in life, love, and business.

THE STORY BEHIND THE BESTSELLER

Most people assume John's first book was *Men Are from Mars, Women Are from Venus*. In reality, that was his third book. His very first, *What You Feel, You Can Heal*, was entirely self-published. John wrote it from a place of deep self-reflection, and even drew his own cartoons to help himself move from one idea to the next. He sold 5,000 copies himself, an incredible achievement for someone with no publisher, no agent, and no marketing team.

John's second book, *Men, Women and Relationships*, took his publishing approach to the next level. By this stage, he had a small distributor who helped him sell 50,000 copies. In those days, that number was remarkable for an independently published book, and it caught the attention of major publishers. They wanted to take the book and republish it under their own banners.

But John's integrity shone through. Even though he had the opportunity to sign with a big publishing house, he chose to stay loyal to the independent distributor who had believed in him early on. That decision still inspires me today, because I know firsthand how much it means when someone gives a small business a chance.

It wasn't until his third book, *Men Are from Mars, Women Are from Venus*, that John signed with a major publisher. That book went on to sell millions of copies, appear on the New York Times bestseller list for several years after publication, and be translated into more than 40 languages. To this day, I still walk into bookstores and see it on the shelves.

And now, full circle, here he is working with me, his first female Mars Venus coach, on our second book together. We first collaborated on *Love and Coaching: Understanding Men and Women in Life, Love and Business*. Now, here we are again, working on *Global Gender Intelligence*. I'm so honored to bring John's words and wisdom, along with the stories of all the new and inspiring Mars Venus coaches around the world, to life.

LESSONS ON WRITING AND SUCCESS

What struck me most in our Bali conversation was John's honesty about writing. He admitted he never thought of himself as a writer. In fact, he found writing difficult, even painful at times. But his purpose to share what he had learned about relationships and self-development through his experience working with couples was more powerful than his resistance.

John's advice to aspiring authors was simple: Don't try to say everything you know in one book. Start with a piece of wisdom, something you could share in an hour-long conversation. Put that into a book, share it, and then listen to the feedback. What do people resonate with? What questions do they ask? That feedback becomes the seed for your next book.

That was exactly John's process. His early works allowed him to refine his ideas. By the time he wrote *Men Are from Mars, Women Are from Venus*, he knew exactly which concepts helped people most. He often told me that books don't succeed because they're long or complicated. They succeed when they're simple, clear, and easy to remember.

THE POWER OF MARKETING YOURSELF

Another powerful lesson John shared was about marketing. Writing a book is only the first step. The real work is getting out there, sharing the message, and embodying it. When John first started, there was no internet or social media. He relied on radio shows, small events, and word of mouth. He said yes to every opportunity, no matter how big or small.

That willingness to back himself was crucial. He didn't wait for success to knock on his door. He created it by saying yes, by showing up, and by consistently sharing his message. As he said, "It's not really selling, it's sharing. And when you share what you are passionate about, success follows." The same is true for coaching or any business.

> **If you're the best-kept secret, your business can't grow because no one knows you exist.**

When I first started coaching, I leveraged John Gray's reputation. People recognized him and his books, and by aligning with the Mars Venus brand, I earned instant trust when I was still unknown. I also shared John's teachings, which gave me valuable content and authority while I was developing my own voice. This helped me grow as a coach and grow my business much faster than I would have if I had tried to do it all as "Susan Dean Coaching."

Back in 2003, coaching itself was new. Most people thought a coach was only for sports! I had to not only enroll clients but also explain what life and relationship coaching was. Today, coaching is far more recognized, but with so many coaches out there, the challenge is standing out. That's where Mars Venus Coaching gives you a unique advantage. Gender intelligence is the differentiator. I'm trained in NLP, hypnosis, and other modalities, but the Mars Venus tools are the most practical and powerful. After all, understanding men and women is essential in relationships, in business, and in life.

I've seen sales teams dramatically increase results by learning how to sell differently to men and women. I've coached companies with my husband Michael where we each worked with men and women separately, then swapped so they could hear from the opposite sex. It completely transformed not only their workplaces but also their home lives.

Over the years, I've coached individuals, couples, businesses, families, teenagers, and even same-sex couples. It doesn't matter who you're working with—the science of Gender intelligence applies to everyone. And when we understand ourselves, our partners, and the people we work with, we create stronger connections, better communication, and greater success in every area of life.

GENDER INTELLIGENCE IN ACTION

Throughout our conversation, John also reminded me that gender differences aren't just theory; they're the foundation of how we live, love, and succeed.

For example, when a man pulls away to reflect or "go into his cave," a woman might assume he's angry or doesn't care. But in truth, he's simply figuring out what to do because he *does* care.

John also talked about how women need affection and emotional connection that isn't always linked to sex. Without this, women can feel rejected or misunderstood. With it, their natural hormones rise, deepening intimacy and passion. These aren't just psychological insights but biological truths, the science of how men and women are wired differently.

And here's where the science gets fascinating:

- **Men under stress** activate the problem-solving part of the brain, often withdrawing to focus or fix.
- **Women under stress** activate the emotional center, seeking connection, reassurance, and empathy.[2]

This is why a man may try to solve problems quickly, while a woman often just wants to be heard. Neither is wrong; they're simply different biological responses.

MENOPAUSE: THE HORMONAL ROLLER COASTER

Of course, these differences become even more pronounced during key life stages, particularly *perimenopause* and *menopause*.

In my late 50s, I entered *that* phase, and let's just say, I was *super sensitive*. Everything Michael did seemed to annoy me, or I struggled to feel like my normal self for a while. And, friends, that wasn't just him being frustrating; it was my hormones running the show.

Science backs this up:
- During *perimenopause*, estrogen levels swing unpredictably, sometimes 20 to 30 percent higher than usual, then suddenly drop.[3]
- These shifts disrupt mood-regulating neurotransmitters like *serotonin* and *dopamine*.[4]
- Studies show that up to *70 percent of women report irritability* as their top symptom during this time,

alongside mood swings, anxiety, and brain fog.[5]
- More than *60 percent of midlife women also report memory and concentration issues*, which adds to the frustration.[6]

No wonder some days I felt like I was losing my mind (and yes, poor Michael copped it when he was just 10 minutes late!). Thankfully, we had the Mars Venus tools and knowledge to understand what was really going on, because the statistics around divorce during this stage of life are frightening. I'm happy to report that Michael made it through unscathed and I can laugh about it now, especially since my daughters nicknamed me "Patricia" during that time (apologies to any Patricias reading this—she was my alter ego, but thankfully she's now long gone!).

The truth is, helping men understand this phase and how they can support their partners through it is absolutely crucial. When a woman feels heard, understood, and supported during these hormonal roller coasters, she comes out the other side even more loving, appreciative, and supportive of her man.

KEY TO SUCCESS—IN MARRIAGE AND BEYOND

What John taught, and what I've lived, is that the key during these times is *understanding, not fixing*.

- **Empathic listening:** A woman doesn't always need

solutions; she needs to be heard and validated.
- **Connection over independence:** Small acts of support, safety, and affection stimulate estrogen, helping a woman's body naturally rebalance.
- **Humor and grace:** Sometimes the best response is a laugh. I often say, "Don't worry, it's menopause, not madness!" Just ask Patricia.

At their core, men just want to please. When they realize it's not about them being "wrong," but about their partners' hormones being in chaos, they can stop taking it personally and instead become their greatest allies.

FULL CIRCLE: STORIES, SUCCESS, AND SHARING

As I reflect on John's journey, I'm reminded of why I do what I do. Just as his first self-published books opened the door to global influence, I know that every author who shares their story has the potential to change lives. A book is never just words on a page. It's transformation, connection, and legacy.

Gender intelligence has shaped my own family life in ways I'll forever be grateful for. When my girls were young and came home upset after a disagreement with their friend at school, my first instinct was to try to fix it. I would suggest what they might have said differently or how they could handle it tomorrow. In truth, I was doing what most men and many mothers naturally do: offer solutions because we don't want our loved ones to feel pain.

Through John's teachings, I learned that what they really needed wasn't advice, but to be heard. So instead of fixing, I simply said: "Sounds like you had a hard day. Come here and give me a hug." That small shift changed everything. It built trust, deepened our bond, and showed my girls I would always be there to listen and support them. And of course, the next day, they were best friends again with the girl they had been upset with.

Those moments, repeated over years, laid the foundation for a close and loving relationship that continues today. Both my daughters now choose to work alongside me in the business, and my youngest even became the youngest certified Mars Venus coach in the world at just 18 years old. Now, as a grandmother to one granddaughter and two grandsons, I continue to see how powerful these principles are across every stage of life. And of course, the Mars Venus teachings have been the foundation of my and Michael's successful 35-year marriage.

But this knowledge hasn't only shaped my family. It has also shaped my work. As a publisher, I guide authors in creating books that build their profile, grow their business, and leave a legacy. As a coach, I help them move through fears, overcome blocks, and stay accountable to their vision. And woven through it all is the foundation of Gender intelligence and the many lessons I learned from John. His teachings are broad and practical—from love and relationships to health, wealth, mindset, and parenting—and they give me tools I can share with authors and clients to support both their personal and professional growth.

> **For me, success has never been only about the business I've built, the coaching I've done, or the books I've published. True success is a life of love and flexibility: a marriage that has lasted decades, a family I get to work and laugh with every day, and the joy of being fully present with my grandchildren. That, to me, is the real science of success in business, love, and life.**

Just as John Gray's teachings have touched millions, my purpose now is to help others share their stories so their wisdom can ripple out into the world. That's the essence of *Global Gender Intelligence*: understanding ourselves, connecting deeply with others, and creating a legacy of love, learning, and lasting impact.

> "The secret of forming a successful relationship is for both partners to win."
>
> **DR. JOHN GRAY**

LIFE IS A LESSON
Embrace Continuous Learning

DR. ABDULRAHMAN AL-DAYEL

Dr. AbdulRahman Al-Dayel is a certified global leader who holds a PhD and master's degree in administrative leadership. He has over 25 years of hands-on experience coaching and training over 17,000 leaders in 73 local and international organizations.

Dr. Al-Dayel coaches and empowers "real leaders" to develop their innate potential and abilities to become better versions of themselves. Focusing on strategic leadership discovery, he has helped many already-successful people become more authentic leaders and achieve institutional excellence.

LEARNING HARD LESSONS IN THE SCHOOL OF LIFE

My life has been a journey of continuous learning. Over 24 years, I have graduated from 14 globally recognized coaching schools and universities. I also hold three master's degrees and completed my doctoral research in leadership management and organizational strategy. Even with all the accreditations, I still consider myself a lifelong learner. In the pursuit of my life's purpose of helping other leaders overcome their challenges, I'm constantly seeking new knowledge and insights, and I reflect that value to others.

My career has been tumultuous, to say the least. Over the years, I left five jobs for various reasons, including injustice, toxic leadership, and my own lack of social intelligence. Ironically, three out of those five former managers are now my coaching and consulting clients, but success did not come easily.

In the workplace, I frequently butted heads with managers who did not understand how to effectively lead their teams. They did not have strong conflict resolution skills, and they did not give us the space to be creative. At the time, in Saudi Arabia, managers received minimal coaching and leadership training. While many knew how to *manage*, few understood how to effectively *lead* a team. In such circumstances, workplace conflict and job dissatisfaction are inevitable.

During one of my most challenging periods, I spent over four years without a stable income. That phase made me realize

I am the captain of my own journey—I am responsible for navigating my life, for *improving* my life. So, with each setback, I pushed forward, learning more, growing more, becoming more. With time, I discovered that my greatest motivation lies in giving, serving humanity, sharing knowledge as a form of intellectual charity, and ultimately transforming lives for the better. I also realized the importance of lowering my expectations of those I work with, which led me to recognize the Mars Venus methodology as one of the most impactful frameworks for my clients—most of whom are leaders in both their professional and personal lives.

As I struggled with setback after setback, the unwavering support of my wife, my mother Ruqayya Al-Saleem, and my younger brother Musaed kept me going. Even a simple smile would inspire me to keep pushing forward. From my most challenging experiences, I learned that, no matter how much strength I try to show, a devoted wife and a nurturing mother are the true pillars of empowerment and resilience.

As my reputation as an executive coach grew, especially after coaching royalty, ministers, and other high-ranking individuals around the world, word got back to some of my former managers. They were interested in my coaching, and three out of five booked sessions with me.

I will admit, those initial sessions were not easy. Here I was working with the same guys who I had clashed with all those years ago. But I knew that anyone could change, and those managers had reached out for a reason. They wanted to change, to grow, to become better in their roles. They did not want to repeat the mistakes of the past. They wanted to be more than managers—they wanted to be authentic leaders.

My most challenging moments and greatest successes reinforced a powerful truth: believe in yourself, trust your abilities, and remain resilient and adaptable.

> **Sometimes, what seems like a loss is actually a redirection toward something greater— but only if you recognize your strengths and seize the opportunity for growth.**

While I learned a lot through formal education, life is the greatest teacher of all. There is no doubt that setbacks come with valuable lessons, and one of the greatest is understanding the true nature of people—something no university or corporate environment can fully teach.

GENDER INTELLIGENCE—THE GATEWAY TO PROFOUND GROWTH

With all the knowledge and qualifications I have amassed over the years, you might be wondering, *Why place the Mars Venus approach on a pedestal?* Surely, it is no more effective than any of the other renowned methodologies I have studied. As an executive coach, mentor, and consultant who has worked with over 17,000 clients in 73 organizations across six continents,

I can say that the Mars Venus approach is critical to success, particularly in the workplace where globalization and industry expansion have introduced diverse perspectives and cultural influences.

The beauty of gender intelligence is *it can be learned.* Once someone realizes it is one of the key factors of success in personal, social, and professional relationships, they naturally recognize the importance of emotional and social intelligence as well. One of the most common traits I have observed in successful leaders is their mastery of gender and emotional intelligence, emphasizing the importance of developing soft skills. These skills play a crucial role in helping individuals achieve their personal and professional goals. Meanwhile, social intelligence ensures a leader's ability to sustain their position and influence within an organization. This principle holds true across all three major sectors—those who rise to the highest leadership positions are often distinguished by their gender intelligence, emotional intelligence, and social intelligence. To cultivate these skills, individuals must first understand their own potential and capabilities, then actively work on acquiring and refining their soft skills. But it all starts with gender intelligence.

LEARN TO LEAD YOURSELF FIRST

When it comes to personal development, the first step is to believe in yourself. Once you have cultivated a healthy level of self-belief, you can work on restoring and strengthening self-confidence. The key is to remain persistent in upholding this confidence while ignoring negativity—no matter how loud those voices may be. This principle is known as *leading yourself before leading others.*

One of the most profound insights I have gained, especially through working with high-ranking individuals, including ministers and royalty worldwide, is that success is primarily determined by how people think.

Their ability to control their thoughts, actively listen, engage in positive self-talk, show empathy, stay true to their values, ask for help when needed, practice humility, manage time and priorities effectively, and care for their mental and physical health are all critical factors. At the core of well-being are structured sleep patterns and a healthy diet—two fundamental pillars of success. Most importantly, knowing when to remain silent and cultivating self-discipline are traits that all great achievers possess.

Being a true and inspiring leader means being a creator of hope, an attentive listener, a motivator, and an enabler, but above all it means *being human.* Studies show that only 10 to 15 percent of successful individuals possess deep awareness of themselves and their capabilities and are driven by ambition and a passion for continuous self-improvement.[7] However, the remaining 85 to 90 percent have faced major setbacks, obstacles, and even heartbreak. It is often these painful experiences that push them beyond their comfort zone into a space of growth, resilience, and continuous development.

Coaching is all about empowerment through experience, and it requires mastering these essential life skills. The ultimate goal is not just to improve the quality of life but to leave a lasting impact that extends beyond one's lifetime.

Once you are ready to embrace personal growth and lifelong learning, you will embark on what I call the Self-Discovery Funnel, which unfolds in three key stages:

- **Explore:** Discover yourself and your passion.
- **Extend:** Expand and sustain your passion and purpose.
- **Enliven:** Rejuvenate your mind, body, and spirit by embracing the meaning of existence.

Commitment to understanding *what you do*, focusing on the skills and abilities you were gifted, and mastering how to apply them is the real path to success. True success lies in turning your journey into meaningful impact.

This concept is deeply rooted in entrepreneurship, where one strives to become a distinctive figure among their peers and contemporaries while staying aligned with core values. It applies to various aspects of life, including:

- Business
- Coaching
- Gender intelligence

- Relationships
- Life fulfillment
- Success
- Love

I want everyone to know that *nothing is impossible as long as your heart is still beating.* Life is a journey—and a short one—so it is essential to seek, and find, your purpose.

UNLOCK YOUR LIMITLESS POTENTIAL

In my professional life, I am committed to being an authentic and genuine leader. I do not compete with others; rather, I challenge myself to grow continuously and step out of my comfort zone into the realm of development. This journey requires self-discipline, humility regardless of success, surrounding oneself with the best minds, and maintaining an unwavering passion for knowledge and continuous self-improvement.

Because I have studied multiple coaching modalities, I am able to coach holistically and adapt to client needs. Flexibility, agility, and relentless effort are key aspects of my approach, but above all, I invest 11 percent of my total income in education to ensure I deliver the best and most valuable insights to my clients. For my efforts, I receive a massive ROI (return on investment), maximizing the impact of my work. This process is also about building a strong reputation, which requires years of dedication, hard work, and limitless giving.

What truly moves me is working with individuals across the age spectrum, ranging from 12 to 98 years old. Despite the wide age range, they all share a common pursuit: the desire to become the best version of themselves. This is incredibly inspiring for high achievers and successful individuals, as it fuels their—and my own—drive for continuous growth and success.

From a continuous learning perspective, the knowledge I gain daily from my coaching clients is some of the most valuable. Among my most inspiring clients is SD from India. She started coaching sessions with me ten years ago, and what makes her journey truly remarkable is that she discovered her potential and capabilities at age 73. For her, it was the beginning of an extraordinary transformation. Over the past decade, she pursued her bachelor's, master's, and doctoral degrees while also launching three entrepreneurial projects—all despite having partial paralysis.

When we first began working together, I was SD's career coach. However, after three sessions, we realized she actually needed a life coach. As it turned out, SD did not need career advice; she needed guidance to change her attitude, perceptions, and behaviors. We have had weekly sessions since 2015, and so far she has achieved every goal she has set for herself, proving that age is just a number. As long as you have passion and drive, which a coach can help cultivate, you can continue to achieve your dreams well into your twilight years. Whether navigating advanced age, a challenging disability, or another perceived barrier, no one should feel like they are out of the game. As SD's story proves, it is never too late to step out of your comfort zone; it is never too late to dream; importantly, it is never too late to achieve those dreams.

A defining trait of successful and accomplished individuals is the journey of self-discovery they have undertaken. This process requires time, effort, and dedication, and the real beauty lies in investing in one's skills and abilities. SD is a living testament to this, and her story demonstrates that self-improvement and growth are limitless.

> "The most effective leaders today are not those who dominate, but those who understand. Emotional intelligence, when combined with gender intelligence, empowers leaders to build trust, motivate authentically, and create environments where everyone thrives."
>
> **DR. JOHN GRAY**

FROM FOOTWORK TO SOULWORK

Reclaim Your Rhythm in Life, Love, and Leadership

SOPHIA KONSTANTINOVNA

Sophia Konstantinovna comes to Mars Venus Coaching with a background as a competitive ballroom and Latin dancer, grassroots entrepreneur, and returned Peace Corps volunteer.

In 2013, she opened the doors to her dance school in Las Vegas, where she quickly became known as the "Dance Doctor." But there was something happening inside the studio that transcended mere footwork. Students were having transformational experiences, not just in posture and poise, but in communication, confidence, chemistry, and a profound sense of renewal and vigor for life.

The studio became a playground for energy exchange, joy, and connection—a place where people could challenge their beliefs about themselves, face their fears, and rediscover what it means to feel truly alive. Couples began reconnecting. Individuals found their spark again. Dance became a secret tool for personal growth and deeper relationships, and a way back to self.

Still, there was something more Sophia wanted to offer: a way to bottle up that magic and make it even more powerful, tangible, and lasting—outside the studio. That's when Mars Venus Coaching entered the picture. The two disciplines dovetailed naturally, and Sophia began weaving Mars Venus Coaching and dancing into her work, expanding her mission to help people improve the quality of their lives through movement, mindset, and relationship insight.

At its core, Sophia's work emanates with palpable urgency, striving to help people reconnect to themselves and each other in a tech-driven world that keeps disconnecting us and draining us of our life force. She offers an elixir of hope, through a variety of modalities, to help people reclaim their natural rhythm in life, love and leadership so they can radiate at their highest capacity in their true God-given design and potential. Her work offers wholeness—in peace, love, and joy.

Now, Sophia's approach bridges the physical and the

psychological, the playful and the profound. What began with ballroom and Latin dance evolved into a multidimensional brand, blending the science of gender intelligence with the art of movement and connection.

Today, she empowers clients worldwide through speaking, coaching, digital programs, and retreats, all under her signature brand: *Sophia in Sapphire*.

A NATURAL STEP IN THE DANCE OF LIFE

My journey into Mars Venus Coaching was a natural step in my purpose-driven life. As a teen, I sat in the back seat of my parents' car, soaking up knowledge from John Gray's Mars Venus tapes. I had an inkling that those ideas would somehow shape my future.

Years later, after serving in the Peace Corps and gaining perspective on life, I came home inspired to follow my dream. In 2013, I opened my ballroom and Latin dance school in Las Vegas—and that's when everything started coming together. I quickly saw that dance wasn't just about movement—it was about transformation. People were reconnecting with each other, healing, and coming alive again.

That's when it all clicked: much of what I witnessed on the dance floor was the Mars Venus philosophy in motion.

In the studio, people weren't just learning footwork—they

were learning confidence, trust, surrender, communication, and so much more. I saw men step into their leadership with purpose, women soften into their feminine, and couples rediscover each other in ways they hadn't in years. The dance floor became a playground for human connection, a space where people shed their fears, rewrote old patterns, and experienced joy like kids again.

But I wanted to take it further and bottle up that magic, making it more tangible outside of the dance studio. Mars Venus Coaching was the perfect complement that allowed me to not only guide people through dance but also help them master the dance of life, love, and communication by understanding the different needs of men and women. This gave me the tools to take the lessons my students were learning on the dance floor and apply them to their relationships, careers, and personal growth. That's when I decided to pivot and weave Mars Venus Coaching into my work, helping people reconnect with themselves and each other both on and off the dance floor.

DANCE TAUGHT ME THE TRUTH ABOUT MEN AND WOMEN

In the early years of my ballroom training, I noticed a pattern: When a man struggled to lead, the woman would either overcompensate or complain. When a woman struggled to follow, the man would either force control or give up. It was never about who was better—it was about understanding the balance of each other's roles, energy, and trust.

Over the years, I saw these same conflicts show up in my students' personal lives. Couples who weren't in sync on the dance floor were often out of sync at home. I could often tell from how they moved together whether a wedding couple had the connection to go the distance. One groom nearly dropped his bride each time he dipped her during the lessons. Although physically strong, every time it came to leading his bride, he zoned out, distracted and disconnected. Turned out, he had a girlfriend on the side.

My single students, on the other hand, often mirrored their uncertainty in dating through a lack of confidence in movement. But when they learned to lead or follow and embraced their masculine or feminine energy, their dating lives exploded.

I'll never forget teaching across from Google in Silicon Valley earlier in my dance career. One of my students came into the studio—a quiet, slouched-over engineer who worked 80 hours per week in front of the computer, depressed, lonely, nerdy, with zero social skills. He signed up for dance lessons, and after a few months, everything changed for him. Learning to lead naturally boosted his testosterone, and he felt great. A new "him" emerged. His posture improved; he started dressing with intention, and suddenly he was asking women to dance … and out on dates with confidence and success. It was a complete 180.

That's when it hit me—it wasn't just about dancing. It

was about the deeper dynamics of men and women: how they show up in the world and to their partners, their energy, their chemistry, and when at their best, the natural flow between them.

I started paying attention beyond the studio. On breaks at cafés, I'd observe how gender intelligence, or a lack of it, was affecting relationships, workplaces, and everyday interactions. I saw women burning out trying to do it all, and men silently struggling to express their needs. And I kept flashing back to those early memories—me in the back seat of my parents' car, listening to John Gray's Mars Venus tapes. His words were now coming to life in my dance lessons.

By this point, it was clear that gender intelligence wasn't just a theory, but a real, measurable key to thriving. That realization changed everything. It elevated my teaching, amplified my impact, and gave my students more than just steps. They were walking away with valuable life skills, relationship tools, and maybe even some secrets of life!

I started becoming known more as a dance doctor than just a dance teacher. I was naturally weaving in concepts of psychology, personal growth, and gender intelligence while helping people transform from the inside out. This is what drew me to the Mars Venus philosophy in the first place. It bridged the gap between science and connection, logic and love.

However, although I witnessed powerful shifts on the dance floor, I didn't fully understand the biology behind it. Men and women are biologically different, and their emotional well-being is deeply tied not just to brain structure, but also to hormones. Testosterone fuels a man's confidence, focus, and drive to provide. Oxytocin fuels a woman's sense of connection, relaxation, and trust. When these hormones are out of balance, relationships suffer. For example, a man needs to feel respected and successful to produce testosterone, which keeps him energized and engaged. But if he feels criticized or micromanaged, his testosterone drops, and he either withdraws or becomes irritable. A woman, on the other hand, thrives when she feels safe, cherished, and supported. That's when oxytocin rises, reducing stress and allowing her to open up. But if she feels overwhelmed, unappreciated, or as if she has to do everything herself, her stress hormone (cortisol) spikes, depleting oxytocin and leaving her exhausted.

With this knowledge, I began encouraging my students to better support each other during dance lessons. I'd remind the women to acknowledge and appreciate the men's efforts, even if they didn't get it right immediately. I also encouraged women to relax into their partners' arms and let them take the lead. Instead of fighting for control, they got permission to let go, stop overthinking, and enjoy not having to call all the shots. It was surprisingly effective—because the suggestions were coming from me, not their partners, which would've likely caused tension. More often than not, it led to laughter as they embraced the challenge, even if it wasn't easy.

When couples understood each other's needs, true partnership began. But when they didn't, they unknowingly triggered stress in each other. When each person fully stepped into their role as leader or follower on the floor, that's when real "dance chemistry" happened and partnerships moved seamlessly as one. I clearly observed the rhythm behind relationships. When gender intelligence is mastered, everything flows.

> **It became clear to me that gender intelligence was the rhythm behind relationships— when you master it, everything flows.**

THE HORMONAL ALCHEMY OF PARTNER DANCING

The term *hormonal alchemy* may sound mystical, but it's rooted in the science of how our bodies and emotions interact. Historically, alchemy was about transforming base metals into gold—taking something common and turning it into something precious.

Similarly, partner dancing acts as a form of alchemy. By embracing our authentic masculine and feminine energy, we trigger the release of healthy hormones, restoring them to optimal levels and stepping into our true selves. This not only boosts our well-being, but also deepens connection and shifts our perspective on life, allowing us to show up as the best versions of ourselves.

When testosterone and oxytocin are in balance, both men and women can meet life's challenges with resilience, show up fully in their relationships, and experience the world through a lens of vitality rather than mediocrity. This shift is powerful. Just as alchemy transforms the ordinary into something extraordinary, honoring our masculine and feminine nature leads to thriving relationships. And dance is absolutely a vehicle that can help us get there.

The dance floor is more than just a space for movement. It's a biological laboratory for stepping into your true self, taking risks, and embracing vulnerability. The movement itself triggers a state change in how we choose to hold ourselves, stand tall, or respond to our partner. Dance shifts our chemistry. It gives us access to a deeper awareness of who we are and a clearer sense of what we bring to a partnership (which is vital). This naturally builds a stronger connection to ourselves and to each other.

For a Man: How Dance Fuels Testosterone and Confidence

Men thrive on testosterone. It's the hormone that makes them feel strong, confident, and purposeful. In today's world, where men are often discouraged from taking the lead or feel unsure about their role, testosterone levels can drop, leaving a man feeling disconnected, passive, or even irritable.

Partner dancing naturally restores a man's testosterone levels by reinforcing his role as a leader, while also allowing him to be present for his partner and feel valued as a result.

- **Leading with clarity and strength:** When a man confidently guides his partner through each movement, his body naturally produces more testosterone. He feels in control, capable, and energized—much like he does when succeeding in other areas of life.

- **Providing stability and direction:** When offering his partner a solid frame and making her feel secure, he taps into his protector-provider instinct, which further fuels his masculinity.
- **Earning a woman's trust and response:** When his partner trusts his lead and responds with grace, it validates his masculinity. The more she surrenders into the dance, the more confident and powerful he feels.

This isn't just an emotional reaction—it's biological. When a man feels needed and respected, his testosterone levels rise. He then becomes more focused, more engaged, and fully present.

For a Woman: How Dance Releases Oxytocin and Relieves Stress

Women, on the other hand, thrive on oxytocin, the bonding hormone, which is the very essence of love, connection, and relaxation. Yet, in today's fast-paced world, women often experience high levels of cortisol (the stress hormone), making them feel overwhelmed, anxious, or emotionally distant.

Partner dancing naturally lowers cortisol levels and boosts oxytocin, creating a profound emotional shift, as well as the following benefits:

- **Being led allows her to relax:** When a woman follows a strong, confident lead, she doesn't have to think or control. She can simply feel. This shift from thinking to feeling lowers cortisol and raises oxytocin, leaving her relaxed, feminine, and deeply connected.
- **Physical touch and connection:** The close embrace while dancing triggers an oxytocin release, just like a warm hug or loving touch. This creates an immediate feeling of safety and bonding.
- **Surrendering to the moment:** When a woman allows herself to be fully present in the dance, moving with the music and her partner, she experiences lightness and freedom. It's a feeling of being cherished and taken care of, exactly what oxytocin thrives on. By letting go and letting her partner lead, she's not just reducing stress hormones, but is reconnecting with her own feminine energy, tapping into the grace and receptivity of her natural rhythm.

A woman who dances with a masculine, confident partner can experience a deep hormonal shift. She walks away feeling more feminine, more connected, and more at peace. This might explain why people get the "dance bug." It can become addictive! The experience we get from dance is like a renewable, natural high—no medication required. Dance *is* medicine. It's the therapy that leads to healthier relationships.

GENDER INTELLIGENCE BEYOND THE DANCE FLOOR

Understanding gender intelligence is about more than mastering dance steps. Through its wisdom, we learn to communicate, connect, and thrive in every area of life.

> **When we embrace the rhythm of the masculine and feminine, we create harmony that reaches far beyond the dance floor.**

This is how we show up for ourselves, for each other, and for the world around us.

What happens on the dance floor is a microcosm of relationships:

- A man who practices leading with confidence in dance finds that this energy carries into his romantic and professional life.
- A woman who learns to let go, trust, and enjoy being led discovers a deeper sense of peace and joy in her relationships.
- Couples who struggle with connection or attraction often find that dancing together reawakens their chemistry in a way that words never could.

This is why the Mars Venus philosophy resonated so deeply with me: it's not just about understanding relationships intellectually; it's about experiencing them in a way that transforms you at a cellular level.

When men and women move together in harmony, when testosterone and oxytocin are at healthy levels as they're meant to be, we don't just exist. We *thrive*. We navigate stress without losing our sanity, and more importantly, we keep our emotional and physical hormonal tanks full enough to connect with our purpose and the people we love. That's how we show up fully, give our best, and ultimately leave a lasting legacy.

MASTER THE DANCE OF YOUR EXTRAORDINARY LIFE

It's essential to recognize a key truth—the life we're conditioned to live is often a limited version of our true God-given potential and human design, keeping us disconnected from our higher purpose. Society may lead us to believe that stress, mediocrity, and disconnection are inevitable, but that doesn't have to be our reality.

Understanding the dynamics between men and women isn't just insightful; it's vital. When we understand each other's needs on a biological, emotional, and energetic level, we move beyond frustration and into deeper connection.

In a world that pulls us in every direction, it's easy to lose sight of what truly matters: our health, our relationships, and our true potential. The answer isn't found in quick fixes. It lies in reconnecting with our most authentic selves, and with each other.

When we embrace understanding, we unlock a life that's aligned with who we truly are. And from that place of balance, everything else begins to fall into place.

This is your invitation: to step into the dance of your life.

Create the life and relationships you've always desired—with clarity, confidence, and purpose.

And next time you're in Vegas, you know where to find me.

The rhythm is within you.

Let it guide you to your highest potential.

> "Balancing hormones is not just a medical concern—it's a relationship essential. When a man is producing healthy testosterone and a woman healthy estrogen, connection flows naturally."
>
> **DR. JOHN GRAY**

ENGINEERING BETTER LIVES

JANEZ ZAVAŠNIK

Janez Zavašnik began his professional career as a master of telecommunications, working for one of the world's largest companies in the field of automated meter reading systems. In his role, he collaborated with $500 million turnover enterprises and international standardization organizations.

After facing several personal and family challenges, Janez encountered the fields of neurolinguistic programming (NLP), hypnosis, and coaching, including Mars Venus. As he explored these disciplines, he was astonished by how little he had previously understood about the deep connection between the brain, language, and human behavior. What fascinated him even more was realizing that the brain and psychology are not purely stochastic or chaotic but grounded in principles and patterns—like the structured logic of engineering and natural sciences he was already familiar with.

Janez completed multiple courses, earning various levels of certification and mastery. Along the way, he immersed himself in books on personal development, life purpose, and partnership—recognizing that human beings are inherently social and embedded in various communities, whether at work, within the family, or in hobbies.

Transitioning from working with devices to working with people, Janez discovered the profound impact of personal transformation—not only on himself as a coachee but also on his loved ones and the wider community.

Janez has been married to his wife Petra for 25 years, and together they have four children.

AN APPROACH GROUNDED IN SCIENCE AND LOGIC

When I first read *Men Are from Mars, Women Are from Venus*, I instinctively felt that the explanations in the book reflected many of the dynamics I was experiencing in my own relationship with my wife. It was eye-opening to realize that what we were going through wasn't unusual—it had patterns and structure.

Years later, when I read *Beyond Mars and Venus*, the concept became even more powerful. The book explored relationship dynamics at the hormonal level, which immediately resonated with me as an engineer. It helped me see that my wife's behavior wasn't just based on mood, upbringing, or personal history; it was also influenced by biology. That scientific understanding was a turning point for me, shifting how I saw our conflicts. Instead of seeing them as clashes between two individuals, I began to view them through the lens of human behavior shaped over thousands of years. It gave us both a new level of respect and compassion, and it helped us work through challenges with greater awareness and mutual support.

Over the past 20 years, neuroscience and hormonal research have advanced dramatically. Today, we're no longer limited to observing differences between men and women based on surface-level behaviors or visible traits; we can now understand those differences at a much deeper level.

Using tools like EEG, MRI, and hormone analysis, science has shown us that many gender-related differences in behavior originate in how our brains function and how our hormones respond in different situations. This means we're not just analysing what happens; we're starting to understand *why* it happens. The most powerful part—this understanding goes beyond analysis; it also offers synthesis. In other words, it gives us actionable guidance. Now we have a scientific foundation for helping men and women behave in ways that are more aligned with their natural hormonal balance and neurological design. When we act in accordance with these insights, we can create healthier, more harmonious relationships, and support both men and women in achieving a state of hormonal homeostasis, where they feel balanced, energized, and fulfilled.

The human brain is the most complex organ in the body, made up of multiple regions and centers responsible for specific behaviors and functions. We can think of the brain as having three main parts: the reptilian brain, the mammalian brain, and the primate brain.

The reptilian brain is primitive and reactive. It produces automatic survival responses like fight, flight, or freeze. The mammalian brain introduces emotion. Mammals act according to their emotional state: when angry, they attack; when afraid, they flee. The primate brain, unique to humans and higher primates, gives us the capacity to reflect, think critically, and observe our emotions rather than just act on them.

Emotions are how our unconscious mind communicates with our conscious mind. Ideally, we should function in a balanced emotional state called homeostasis, where the brain and body work in harmony and we feel generally positive and stable. Our bodies constantly aim to maintain this state. However, life inevitably brings stress. When we're under pressure but still managing, we shift into allostasis—a state where we appear to function normally, but only by drawing on internal reserves. This requires more effort, making us feel more tired or depleted over time. If the stress continues or increases and our resources are no longer enough, something gives. We may feel emotional pain, experience burnout, or even become physically ill.

This kind of mindfulness—being aware of which part of the brain is currently in charge—helps us stay out of autopilot. It keeps us from being driven by pure instinct or emotion. While operating from our higher human mind requires mental effort (and yes, sometimes discomfort), it brings deep satisfaction. It's the path to living not just reactively, but consciously, as a human being fully present and fully alive.

Often, however, it's easier said than done, which is why seeking support is crucial. People can find themselves in negative emotional situations so intense that emotional pain appears. Some people can feel this as a physical pain, but the majority of people don't. Even though they don't feel the physical pain, they act as if they do: they isolate themselves, withdraw from activity, and avoid even small tasks, because any additional effort seems to deepen their pain. Some try to push forward and "fix" things right away, but problem-solving is the second step. The first step is to learn how to solve the problem.

That might sound like a small detail, but in my view, it's crucial. Without the right knowledge or skills, solutions remain out of reach. When someone keeps trying to solve a problem without success, their frustration can grow even stronger. That's why the true beginning is gaining the necessary knowledge and skills that make problem-solving possible. Sometimes, the simplest—but also the hardest—step is to ask for help from a coach. That small act of reaching out can be the turning point.

Understanding this helps us reframe both positive and negative emotions. A positive emotion signals that something good is happening, but too much stimulation (for example, ecstasy, overexcitement) can become dangerous. In such cases, we should use our conscious mind and try to return to balance by pulling ourselves back down. Similarly, a negative emotion signals that something needs attention. Instead of being overwhelmed by it, we can pause, reflect, and rationally identify its cause. Then we can take action to reduce or eliminate that cause or at least find ways to manage it better.

As an engineer, the logic and scientific grounding of gender intelligence appealed to me, so when I switched careers—from telecommunications to coaching—I decided to add the Mars Venus methodology to my repertoire. I was searching for a niche to specialize in, and I already had some experience coaching people around relationships. During my coaching training, my wife and I were invited to assist a lecturing coach by preparing sub-courses focused on partnership, combining our newly acquired knowledge and skills with the experiences gained from our long-term marriage. With gender intelligence added to my repertoire, I had finally found my niche.

RELATIONSHIPS AREN'T A LOTTERY

Many people treat finding and living with a partner like a lottery. They imagine an ideal partner, someone who won't expect them to change at all and will love and accept them even in their most difficult moments. But when the relationship doesn't meet those expectations, they often feel it's time to "draw again" and start over, chasing the romantic ideal.

But real relationships aren't based on luck. A healthy partnership should be seen as a long-term commitment where both partners are responsible, first for themselves and then for the shared aspects of life like household responsibilities, finances, and parenthood. One of the most important truths is that life will bring challenges—some that affect just one partner and others that impact the relationship as a whole.

> **In challenging moments, true partners are the ones who commit to work—investing their time, energy, and money—through those challenges together.**

Maintaining a healthy relationship often requires something many people overlook in their personal lives: the willingness to grow. We're used to investing in personal development for our careers, but rarely do we apply the same mindset to our relationships. And yet, developing new knowledge and emotional skills—what we call personal growth—is exactly what's needed to build a lasting, fulfilling partnership.

The truth is, your partner doesn't have to be "perfect." What matters most is that you share core values, take responsibility for your individual lives, and both commit to contributing to the relationship over the long term.

GENDER INTELLIGENCE—A GAME CHANGER IN BUSINESS

Gender intelligence applies to more than just romantic partnerships; it also applies to business. In high-performance and highly competitive environments, it's important that we understand the influence of gender-based traits. While differences between men and women are often subtle, they tend to become more noticeable at the extreme ends of certain traits and in areas that demand intense competition or physical performance.

Take height, for example. On average, men are about 7 percent taller than women.[8] But when we look at the extreme high end, the tallest recorded woman reached 215 cm (7 feet 1 inch), while the tallest man was 272 cm (8 feet 11 inches).[9] Above 215 cm, all individuals are male. This kind of statistical trend appears in many domains—not as a value judgment, but as a natural outcome of biological distribution.

Similarly, in professional sports, victory often hinges on the smallest margins. In the Tour de France, a grueling three-week cycling race, the winner may beat the runner-up by just a fraction of the total time, yet the winner takes all the recognition.

In such elite environments, even a small advantage in certain traits can make a large difference.

In business, especially in very competitive and high-pressure fields, certain traits—like aggression, risk-taking, and single-focus attention—are generally more prevalent in men. That doesn't mean women can't succeed in those environments—they absolutely can—but it often requires greater effort or energy because the environment may not naturally align with their gender-specific strengths. This is why understanding gender intelligence is so important. It allows both individuals and organizations to recognize that success isn't just about pushing harder; it's also about aligning roles and environments with people's innate strengths. It's not about limiting anyone; it's about increasing awareness so everyone can thrive by working with, not against, their natural tendencies.

A PRACTICAL APPROACH TO COACHING

When people first come to me, they're often operating as if they're trapped in a car, pushing the gas pedal as hard as possible but without putting the car in gear. All the energy they invest only results in increased engine temperature, with no other effect. They're eager to leave the place where they currently find themselves, but they have no clear destination and no plan for the journey ahead.

As a coach, my first step is to help them stop for a moment—take their foot off the gas. We pause to create clarity:

"Where do you really want to go?"

"What obstacles are standing in the way?"

"What new knowledge and skills do you need to reach your goal?"

Only then can we put the car into first gear and begin moving forward, slowly, intentionally, one step at a time. Speed isn't important—it's progress that matters most.

My engineering background strongly influences my coaching approach. I'm focused, rational, and practical. I help clients shift from reacting emotionally to responding thoughtfully. We work on moving from the emotional part of the brain to the rational part—because when emotions settle, people can begin to take practical steps forward. And practical change requires knowledge and skills. That's where coaching tools and techniques come in. I guide people in developing real-life abilities to navigate both personal and professional challenges more effectively.

Today, compared to the past, people generally have more knowledge and skills—and more tools are available—to navigate relationships. Yet paradoxically, they also experience more challenges in their partnerships. This reflects the reality that societal expectations and pressures on modern relationships are far more demanding than they were 30 or more years ago.

Let's consider how people actually spend their lives: in an average 80-year lifespan, a person might spend around 30 years sleeping or trying to fall asleep, 15 years working, 4 years eating, 6 years in front of screens, 4 years on transport, 5 years socializing, 5 years managing household duties, 6 years on parenting, 2 years in education, and 1 year exercising. That leaves just about 2 years for everything else, including personal time with a partner. Despite this, people tend to place enormous emotional weight on their partnerships, often judging their overall life satisfaction through the lens of their romantic relationships. When they're unhappy, people may assume it's because their relationship is flawed, when it may actually be the stress from other life domains seeping in.

I once worked with a couple experiencing exactly this. On the surface, it appeared their relationship was failing. The wife frequently said things like, "You never tell me you love me" or asked, "Please, hug me." Her tone often carried stress, frustration, and emotional tension. The husband, meanwhile, interpreted these requests as blame—he felt accused of not doing enough, despite his ongoing efforts. He believed his contributions should be sufficient, especially since they had once been enough earlier in the relationship. At first, what neither realized was that the root of the issue wasn't the relationship itself; it was external stress, especially from work, that was unconsciously being brought into their home. The wife, under constant stress, was subconsciously seeking relief and emotional support from her husband, hoping he would help reduce her anxiety through presence, affection, and validation.

Through coaching, we explored two key aspects: first, how the wife could recognize and self-regulate her stress more effectively, and second, how the husband could better understand her needs without internalizing them as personal criticism. With these insights, the couple realized that their partnership wasn't broken at all. In fact, it had a strong foundation, but there had been misinterpretations due to unspoken stress and mismatched expectations. Once they shifted their understanding, they began to support each other more consciously, leading to a deeper connection and renewed appreciation for their relationship.

Sometimes, unconditional love is overrated, especially when it leads to one person continuously giving without considering their own well-being. Even rescuers and lifeguards are taught to prioritize their own safety first before helping someone else. I believe we should apply the same wisdom to how we love.

> **If we want to give love to someone else, we must first have it within ourselves. Ideally, we give from a place of abundance, not scarcity. Only then can our love truly support others, without harming ourselves in the process.**

It's important to remember that we live our lives first and foremost for ourselves, and then for others. Trying to give something we don't have is like taking out a loan from the bank to give money to someone else. No matter how noble the intent, we're the ones who have to pay the interest—emotionally, physically, or spiritually. Over time, this can lead to burnout, resentment, or bitterness when we feel we're always giving while receiving nothing in return.

On the flip side, we must also train ourselves to receive. Love isn't always grand gestures. Sometimes, it comes in the form of a smile, a kind word, or a quiet look in the eyes. When we recognize and appreciate these moments, they can feel more valuable than anything money can buy.

Ultimately, love—like many meaningful things in life—works best when it's multiplicative. When both people contribute with care and intention, the result becomes greater than the sum of its parts. True love isn't about sacrifice alone; it's about creating a shared space where both people grow, feel nourished, and become more than they could be alone.

As a coach, I face the ongoing challenges of helping clients stay committed through discomfort. Growth isn't always pleasant, but I've found that when we focus on small, manageable steps and build skills incrementally, even the biggest changes become possible.

ASK GOOD QUESTIONS, RECEIVE GOOD ANSWERS

There are many valuable concepts and techniques that contribute to effective coaching, but the most important element, in my view, is the ability to ask good questions. What makes a question "good" in coaching? It's not about giving answers or leading someone in a specific direction. Good questions create space for the coachee to gradually gain awareness of their challenges, of the internal or external blocks they face, and of the new knowledge or skills they may need to move forward. These gradual insights are key to success. They allow the coachee to realize that progress isn't something given by the coach, but something they're creating for themselves. This shift in perspective is crucial—because only when the coachee fully owns the process can real personal growth happen.

The power of coaching lies not in advice, but in awakening a person's ability to think differently, act with intention, and take responsibility for their journey.

HAPPINESS ISN'T THE GOAL

As we walk the path of growth and self-development, it's important to know that the purpose of life isn't to be happy—happiness is the result of something deeper.

Life will always bring challenges. That's why I believe the true purpose of life is to gain experience, and when problems arise, our task is to either solve them or, if they can't be solved, to accept them. As the famous saying goes (credited to several thinkers): "Grant me the serenity to accept the things I cannot change, the courage to change the things I can, and the wisdom to know the difference."

When we do the inner and outer work to find solutions—regardless of the time, energy, or suffering involved—we often discover a deeper, more grounded form of happiness on the other side. It's not fleeting pleasure; it's the fulfillment that comes from growth, resilience, and purpose.

Some people believe happiness means a life without effort—physical, emotional, or spiritual. They may even interpret ease as a sign of divine favor, but life doesn't work that way. If we don't adapt and grow in response to what life brings, we fall behind, and when we fall behind, we often experience even deeper frustration and dissatisfaction.

True happiness comes after growth, not instead of it, and success in life isn't about being the best; it's about being honest with ourselves. Can we say we gave our best, based on our current capabilities, values, and circumstances? Did we invest all we could, without compromising who we are?

We're not almighty, and true success often lies in the peace that comes from knowing we did our part fully, regardless of the outcome.

> "Hormonal differences aren't just biological—they shape how we think, feel, and respond to stress. When we understand the science behind our differences, we can stop blaming and start understanding."
>
> **DR. JOHN GRAY**

UNLOCK EXCLUSIVE BONUS CONTENT!

Dr. John Gray and his certified coaches have created powerful resources to enhance your understanding of gender intelligence and the wider Mars Venus philosophy.

Inside your free bonus pack, you'll get:
- Audio downloads
- Printable worksheets
- Practical tools and resources—and more!

Visit **marsvenuscoaching.com/bookbonus** to access your bonuses now.

GENDER INTELLIGENCE IS THE FUTURE

MAIBA MARINO

Maiba Marino is an author, music producer, and life and relationship coach from Munich, Germany.

After studying linguistics and literature, she traveled frequently and lived abroad, gaining a deeper understanding of the world and the people in it. Maiba speaks several languages and is highly interested in foreign cultures.

Later trained in audio production, she began living her passion for music and creativity, frequently performing at music events and writing new songs in the studio.

Due to her active lifestyle, Maiba understands the importance of a healthy and balanced diet. She also knows that harmonious relationships contribute significantly to our general well-being.

Through gender-intelligent coaching, Maiba helps others gain clarity and empathy, guiding them to better understand themselves and the opposite gender, bringing balance to their lives (and love lives). She strongly believes that good health and fulfilling relationships don't happen by coincidence; they're the result of choosing to take our lives into our own hands. Therefore, Maiba's mission is to inspire and support as many people as possible to create their ideal lifestyles, build better relationships, and become the best versions of themselves.

ROLE MATES OR SOUL MATES ... WHY NOT BOTH?

When I started coaching, I realized people are confused about how the world has changed and frustrated about not knowing their role and function in relationships. Many guys complain that they feel confused about the role reversal of men and women. They think women have ridiculous expectations of men nowadays. Men of all ages and cultures are overwhelmed by the new-won power of modern women, with females entering and excelling in the business world. Some men even feel threatened by the change, turning their frustration into hatred toward women. The hatred is evident online but also in the workplace and in daily interactions between men and women. I consider it a serious issue.

Not only is it a serious issue, but it's also a constant challenge I face in my gender intelligence coaching. While my original goal was to help women—because I truly believe in women empowerment—I also support men, especially those who feel threatened or confused by women. I help them accept our changing world and our shifting roles within it. Through men overcoming their egos and being more empathetic toward women, both genders can find peace. That's why my long-term goal is to contribute to helping the world overcome competition and misunderstanding between men and women so we can meet at eye level, make peace with the opposite sex, become the best versions of ourselves, and live fulfilling lives.

In my opinion, it's crucial to show men that women are overwhelmed and confused too. Modern women doing what were traditionally considered male jobs are facing immense pressure. At work, they're competing with men and working like men, and when they get home, they're often expected to take over household responsibilities while being loving wives and mothers. For many women, it's a stressful situation, and when women are stressed, they can lean too far toward their male side (high testosterone, low estrogen). If they don't address the problem and raise their estrogen and oxytocin levels, they'll remain unbalanced, feeling overwhelmed and unable to return to their loving and nurturing side, always putting too much on their plate and eventually getting burned out.

One of my female clients was being bullied at work. Due to conflict with her direct boss, who was preventing her from climbing the corporate ladder, my client felt limited in her career. Her boss constantly blamed her for issues outside of her control and was threatening her with job loss. Unfortunately, in German job culture, experiences like this are common.

So, how did I help my client?

Firstly, I considered if it were possible to include her boss in our coaching sessions. We decided this wasn't an option. My client's boss was dealing with depression, showing signs of burnout, and wasn't keen on adding another task to his to-do list.

I decided to approach the issue from another angle. Instead of trying to change the boss's opinion and behavior toward my client, I worked to change my client's energy state and mindset. By applying certain Mars Venus coaching tools, combined with resolving emotional blocks, we managed to dissolve the resentment she had toward her boss. I also helped my client see the situation from her boss's perspective so she could better understand the source of the conflict. We also worked on her fear of the future and financial problems by discussing her options so she could free her mind from being stuck in analysis paralysis and rather focus on being confident and aware of her capabilities. With this new energy state, she returned to work ready to face whatever came her way.

The result? My client didn't get fired. While the situation wasn't perfect—there were still some obstacles to overcome—the tone and energy in the workplace changed for the better.

To combat toxic workplace cultures, new ways of thinking and new relationship and communication tools are required, learning to see one another as complimentary and not competitory. We should embrace how the world has developed, yet be aware that the interdependence of men and women still exists and is crucial to the functioning of society.

Having traveled a lot and even lived abroad for long periods of my life, I speak different languages and have always been open to other cultures. I'm very interested in how other countries approach male-female dynamics. It will be interesting to see how the Mars Venus philosophy is accepted in the Middle East and how role reversals of Western countries gradually merge into these cultures.

Muslim societies are still holding on to the role mate principles, which have their benefits, but they aren't so easy to fulfill anymore, as the world has changed. In the Western world, with men and women both established in the business world, they don't depend on one another so much anymore. While this leads to greater freedom, it can also cause confusion and overwhelm. Merging these two approaches to life and relationships, combining the best of both worlds, can help bring men and women closer together. Because ultimately, we can be role mates and soul mates at the same time.

FINALLY, IT ALL MADE SENSE!

For many years, I've been interested in health and relationships. I even studied nutrition and health coaching and now coach others to improve their lifestyles. Throughout my life, I've experienced many of the challenges my clients face, overcoming my own health issues brought on by high stress levels, poor lifestyle habits, and a painful divorce. Over the years and through my training, I've learned the importance of proper nutrition, living an active lifestyle, and maintaining good relationships. Ultimately, healthy habits and leading a balanced life contribute positively to our overall well-being. Because I can relate so strongly to my clients' stories, I'm able to better guide them and provide them with the tools and strategies I know work—because they worked for me.

> **Stress, unhealthy habits, and lack of communication in relationships often lead to misunderstandings and frustration on both sides. With the right health strategies and knowledge around how men and women cope with stress, we can all live healthy and fulfilling lives.**

When my marriage fell apart during the pandemic, I realized how misunderstanding and miscommunication between couples often pave the way for relationships ending, and I didn't want to repeat the mistakes of the past. *Men are from Mars, Women are from Venus* sat on my bookshelf for many years, ignored and unread. During my separation, the book stayed with me (maybe it was destiny), and I decided the time had come to finally read it.

What an amazing book! I was blown away by the obvious facts Dr. John Gray explained. I bought some of his other books too, going down the rabbit hole and learning more each day. Finally, when the opportunity arose to become a Mars Venus coach, I didn't think twice. Because I was already coaching people around health and nutrition, the Mars Venus methodology seemed like the ideal complement—and I was right!

> **When you study the Mars Venus Coaching philosophy, you grow to truly understand the differences between the male and female brain, how we're wired, and how we respond differently to certain things. You develop empathy for the other gender, for friends, family members, and even yourself.**

For me, learning about men's and women's hormonal cycles and how they're linked to our stress levels was a game changer. So much of our behavior finally made sense. Applying the Mars Venus methodology to my own life positively impacted all of my relationships. Just knowing you can influence your hormones without the need for artificial hormonal replacements is invaluable. Ultimately, happy hormones lead to happy relationships and, therefore, a happier and healthier life.

THE QUEST OF BALANCE

Due to my background in health and nutrition, I coach holistically, knowing that general well-being starts with a healthy body and mind. Before you can begin working on achieving your dreams or attracting the ideal partner, you must get your house in order. Therefore, I always include health and nutrition in my coaching, which gets consistently positive results for my clients.

While coaching men, I discovered that if a man gets stressed out from work or life in general, his testosterone level drops, and he develops various symptoms like fatigue, sluggishness, irritability, depression, and overwhelm. He also turns more toward his feminine side, and his estrogen level rises. It can even lead a relatively young man to not have sex with his wife or any other women for a prolonged period.

One male client I helped was suffering from severe stress. Through coaching, I guided him to rebalance his body and mind. First, the client went through an intense personal coaching period with me for several months. We worked on multiple problems in his personal life. It turned out he was very much on his female side, giving more than he should (and could) to all the people around him (family, wife, boss). As a result, he often felt overwhelmed and exhausted, and had no passion or libido. After I recommended a checkup with his doctor, due to some minor health issues, he learned he needed to change his diet. So, I created a diet plan for him and set him up with some supplements to boost his immune system and energy levels.

We also created a plan to structure more "me time" for him and also more "we time" with his wife. I recommended that they do more physical activities together—for example, they both started going to the gym.

Soon, my client was back in his male energy and felt more in charge of his health and time. As a result, not only did he feel better, but he also stopped complaining (which raises estrogen levels in a man instead of boosting testosterone!). He began focusing on people and activities that were priorities in his life, and he learned to say "no" when friends or family members asked too much of him. Not only did he value himself more, but people also appreciated him more. Eventually, he felt renewed love and attraction toward his wife, and was willing to give his love life another chance.

In our not-allowed-to-fail society, stress and overwork are a problem. People push themselves to achieve more in less time until they burn out and can't help feeling like a failure. Wouldn't it be much better if we didn't put so much on our agendas? Wouldn't it be great if we celebrated and took pride in our smaller achievements? Wouldn't it be ideal if we could make mistakes and learn from them without feeling like losers? With the right tools and guidance, we can achieve all this and more.

Another client of mine, a woman, realized through my coaching how much her hormonal imbalance was affecting her relationship with her partner. In the days before her period, she acted out in very disturbing ways, sometimes even in front of people, and caused a scene that, in the end, led to huge fights and tears. Only when I explained to her what happens inside her did she understand that there was nothing wrong with *her*; the problem related to her hormones.

Hormonal imbalance is still totally underestimated in terms of its connection to not only our overall well-being but also our ability to build and maintain good relationships. If we pay more attention to how women and men are different, not only in looks and behaviors but also in hormone levels, we can find ways to cope more effectively with stress. When men and women learn to balance their stress levels and come back to their authentic side, it brings them closer to each other, creating a more loving relationship.

LOVE IS ALL WE NEED ... ALMOST

Relationships are a major part of life, yet nobody is taught in school what it really takes to build and maintain good relationships. Parents can't be good examples either if they haven't been taught the proper skills.

I believe that *Beyond Mars and Venus: Relationship Skills for Today's Complex World* should be mandatory reading in every school, as it's the key to teaching great relationship and communication skills, while at the same time teaching us to take care of our own needs.

In my opinion, gender intelligence is the future. It can

system and energy levels.

We also created a plan to structure more "me time" for him and also more "we time" with his wife. I recommended that they do more physical activities together—for example, they both started going to the gym.

Soon, my client was back in his male energy and felt more in charge of his health and time. As a result, not only did he feel better, but he also stopped complaining (which raises estrogen levels in a man instead of boosting testosterone!). He began focusing on people and activities that were priorities in his life, and he learned to say "no" when friends or family members asked too much of him. Not only did he value himself more, but people also appreciated him more. Eventually, he felt renewed love and attraction toward his wife, and was willing to give his love life another chance.

In our not-allowed-to-fail society, stress and overwork are a problem. People push themselves to achieve more in less time until they burn out and can't help feeling like a failure. Wouldn't it be much better if we didn't put so much on our agendas? Wouldn't it be great if we celebrated and took pride in our smaller achievements? Wouldn't it be ideal if we could make mistakes and learn from them without feeling like losers? With the right tools and guidance, we can achieve all this and more.

Another client of mine, a woman, realized through my coaching how much her hormonal imbalance was affecting her relationship with her partner. In the days before her period, she acted out in very disturbing ways, sometimes even in front of people, and caused a scene that, in the end, led to huge fights and tears. Only when I explained to her what happens inside her did she understand that there was nothing wrong with *her*; the problem related to her hormones.

Hormonal imbalance is still totally underestimated in terms of its connection to not only our overall well-being but also our ability to build and maintain good relationships. If we pay more attention to how women and men are different, not only in looks and behaviors but also in hormone levels, we can find ways to cope more effectively with stress. When men and women learn to balance their stress levels and come back to their authentic side, it brings them closer to each other, creating a more loving relationship.

LOVE IS ALL WE NEED ... ALMOST

Relationships are a major part of life, yet nobody is taught in school what it really takes to build and maintain good relationships. Parents can't be good examples either if they haven't been taught the proper skills.

I believe that *Beyond Mars and Venus: Relationship Skills for Today's Complex World* should be mandatory reading in every school, as it's the key to teaching great relationship and communication skills, while at the same time teaching us to take care of our own needs.

In my opinion, gender intelligence is the future. It can

form the foundation of every relationship (business, romance, family, friendships, politics). If we taught gender intelligence in school, it would lead to more respectful and educated people and, therefore, a better world.

Love is all we need—the Beatles were almost right when they sang those words, even if it sounds cliché. In truth, love isn't *all* we need, but it is what we most need in life. If we all came from a more loving place, it would improve our lives in the most amazing way.

> "The future of our relationships, our families, and even our global cooperation depends on how well we embrace gender intelligence. Teaching these principles early and widely is essential for the next generation to thrive."
>
> **DR. JOHN GRAY**

A LIFE BUILT ON GENDER INTELLIGENCE

DR. MICHAEL-RAY DEAN

Dr. Michael-Ray Dean is an internationally recognized Mars Venus coach and gender intelligence thought leader. With over 20 years of international experience in the coaching field, he has built a seven-figure coaching enterprise and trained coaches worldwide, multiplying the ripple effect of gender intelligence into countless lives, relationships, and organizations.

Michael-Ray isn't just a coach but also an engineer pilot, elite bodyguard and close protection agent, jujitsu practitioner, covert operative specialist, NATO-accredited firearms and hostile environment combat specialist, and certified combat medic. He also holds a Doctorate in Science specializing in human behavior. With his unique combination of skills and decades of real-world experience, he clinically reverse engineers his clients' outcomes into step-by-step strategies that consistently outperform expectations and set him apart from others in his field.

From his sanctuary—a 10-acre estate nestled in the foothills of the Australian mountains—where he works with his wife Susan, Michael-Ray operates his international coaching and consulting practice while embodying the very principles of balance, connection, and purpose he teaches.

A JOURNEY OF INSIGHT AND UNDERSTANDING

When I look back on my journey—three decades of marriage to my teenage sweetheart Susan, raising two strong daughters, and now stepping into the role of "Pa" to three grandchildren—one thread runs through it all: *gender intelligence*.

In the early years, I thought I had marriage figured out. I worked hard; I provided; I fixed problems as they arose. If Susan seemed upset, I would jump straight in with solutions. If one of my daughters was struggling at school, I would offer strategies. To me, this was love in action. I was doing what a man should do: protect, provide, solve.

But I didn't realize that my good intentions were creating distance. Susan didn't always want me to fix her problems; she wanted me to hear her. My daughters didn't always want strategies; they wanted support. To me, listening without fixing felt like *doing nothing*. To them, it meant everything.

It took years of trial and error before I finally grasped the deeper truth that Dr. John Gray explains in *Men Are from Mars, Women Are from Venus*: men instinctively try to fix, while women instinctively seek connection. My instinct to provide solutions wasn't wrong, but it was often counterproductive. What my family truly needed was presence, not performance.

The shift happened slowly. I began experimenting with simply listening, holding back the urge to fix. To my surprise, the results were dramatic. Susan felt more supported; our daughters' confidence grew, and I realized that real strength isn't measured by how fast I can solve problems, but by how deeply I can connect. Ultimately, men become stronger partners and fathers when they learn to balance fixing with listening.

As men, our drive to provide and protect is fueled not just by instinct but also by biology. Testosterone gives us energy, focus, and the will to achieve. Dopamine gives us the reward of accomplishment and progress. When those hormones are fueled in healthy ways, men rise as leaders, protectors, and role models. When they're pursued through unhealthy habits, men spiral into distraction, dependency, and disconnection.

In my coaching, I've seen both paths. Some men transform their families by channeling their energy into building businesses, advancing careers, exercising discipline, caring for their health, and cultivating meaningful hobbies. Others lose themselves to quick dopamine hits: alcohol, drugs, pornography, endless social media scrolling. These behaviors rob them of vitality, weaken their relationships, and erode trust. Healthy masculinity means choosing habits that build strength and stability. While quick fixes may feel good for a moment, they destroy confidence in the long run.

Just as men thrive on testosterone, women are naturally energized and restored by oxytocin—the hormone of love, connection, and bonding. When oxytocin is replenished in healthy ways, women feel balanced, confident, and capable of giving and receiving love. When it's depleted or replaced by unhealthy dopamine-releasing habits, women can feel overwhelmed, anxious, and disconnected from their true selves.

I've seen women flourish when they embrace healthy oxytocin generators: meaningful conversations with loved ones, nurturing connections, acts of self-care, creative expression, giving and receiving affection, and spiritual practices. These habits restore balance and enhance a woman's natural radiance.

I've also seen what happens when women rely on unhealthy dopamine-releasing substitutes: endless scrolling for validation, compulsive shopping, emotional eating, numbing with alcohol. These quick hits soothe temporarily but leave women feeling more drained. True feminine strength isn't about doing more; it's about filling your own tank with healthy oxytocin so you can give from a place of abundance.

Whether you're a man or a woman, understanding gender intelligence can enhance every aspect of your life. Gender differences impact not just relationships, but also stress management, performance, and overall health. When you respect and integrate these differences, success comes more easily.

TRUE DEFINITION OF SUCCESS

As a younger man, I equated provision with money. If I worked hard, paid the bills, and created opportunities for my family, I believed I was fulfilling my role. I believed I was successful. On one level, yes, financial provision matters, but I was blind to the fact that success has multiple dimensions.

For many years, I defined success in narrow terms: job titles, income, achievements. I was focused on building, achieving, and proving. And while those accomplishments mattered, there came a point where I realized something was missing. I had the outward results, but inside there was still a void.

The breakthrough came when I began to see that true success isn't only about reaching goals. Dr. John Gray defines success as "getting what you want and wanting what you have." That truth resonates deeply with me.

Before I discovered and applied the Mars Venus philosophy

to my own life, there were seasons when I was so consumed by work that I came home physically present but emotionally absent. Susan longed for connection, but I was still in my "cave," replaying business problems in my head. I thought, *Why isn't she happy? I'm doing this for us.* I couldn't see that my emotional absence had created a void in our relationship.

The turning point came when I redefined provision and, in turn, success. Provision isn't just financial. It's emotional, relational, and spiritual. Susan didn't need me only as a provider of income; she needed me as a provider of presence, support, and safety. I realized that family dinners, Susan's smile, and holidays with loved ones mattered just as much as any business result. When I was consumed by work, I missed too many of those simple yet profound moments. However, rebalancing taught me they weren't "extras"; they were the essence of success. When I started to listen, to show up emotionally, and to share my time intentionally, our marriage flourished in ways money alone could never achieve.

THE UNIVERSALITY OF GENDER INTELLIGENCE

Throughout my coaching career, I've worked across continents, with executives in Asia, entrepreneurs in Europe, and leaders in Australia. Cultures vary; languages differ; and industries shift. Yet one principle remains constant: men and women are wired differently, and those differences matter everywhere. Gender intelligence is universal because biology is universal.

I've seen male executives withdraw under stress, believing silence is strength, while female colleagues interpret that silence as rejection. I've seen female leaders process challenges by talking them through, only to be judged as "indecisive" by male peers wired to look for rapid solutions. These aren't failures of character; they're failures of interpretation.

> **Our differences aren't problems; they're patterns, and when understood, they become tools for connection rather than sources of conflict.**

When leaders learn to recognize these patterns rather than take them personally, everything changes. Teams communicate better. Decisions improve. Respect grows.

GENDER INTELLIGENCE ISN'T JUST FOR ADULTS

I see gender differences every time I'm with my grandchildren. My grandsons are drawn to trucks, cars, and anything that crashes or roars. They want to build forts, climb trees, and push boundaries. My granddaughter, by contrast, gravitates toward dolls, dress-ups, and games of connection. She naturally looks for ways to nurture, to relate, to include.

No one told them to behave that way. No one forced toys

into their hands. These tendencies simply emerged—and that's the beauty of it. Our kids are living proof that Dr. John Gray's teachings aren't just theory, but observable reality. Boys and girls are wired differently, and when honored, these differences aren't limitations; they become strengths.

By honoring gender differences early, we set the stage for confidence later in life. Instead of trying to neutralize children, encourage them to explore their natural tendencies. Celebrate differences as strengths. A boy who learns to channel his drive becomes a focused man. A girl who learns to embrace her connection becomes a grounded woman.

One of the greatest privileges of my life has been raising daughters. From the time they were young, I realized my role wasn't only to protect them; it was to show them what they should expect from a man. Every word I spoke, every action I took toward their mother, and every choice I made was subtly setting the bar for the men they would one day invite into their lives.

If I treated Susan with respect, kindness, and consistency, my daughters grew up believing that was normal. If I listened to her, supported her, and honored her, they learned that those qualities weren't luxuries, but essentials. The reverse is also true: if I had dismissed, belittled, or neglected Susan, that would have set a far lower standard.

I'm proud to say that today my daughters have chosen good men, partners who reflect the values they saw modeled at home. It's no coincidence. When daughters grow up feeling worthy, loved, and respected, they don't settle for less.

While I haven't raised sons myself, the principles Dr. John Gray outlines in *Men Are from Mars, Women Are from Venus* apply powerfully to boys as they grow into men. Boys are naturally driven by testosterone. They want to compete, achieve, and prove themselves. But unless they're guided, those instincts can become reckless or self-centered. Fathers and mothers alike play a vital role in shaping how boys learn to honor and respect women.

From an early age, boys should be taught that domination isn't strength. True masculinity is shown in protecting, providing, and respecting. When a boy sees his father open doors for his mother, listen to her, and speak with kindness, he absorbs that model. When he experiences his mother setting healthy boundaries and his father honoring them, he learns that respect is nonnegotiable.

When boys see that real men honor their commitments, listen before speaking, and treat women with dignity and respect, they become men who elevate the women in their lives rather than diminish them.

If you're a parent, ask yourself: *What standard am I setting for my children?* The way you treat your partner, the way you handle stress, and the respect you show all become the blueprint your kids unconsciously carry into their future relationships.

GLOBAL IMPACT OF GENDER INTELLIGENCE

My journey—from engineer to pilot, from martial artist to close protection agent, from combat medic to behavioral scientist and gender intelligence coach—has taught me one truth: *Skills alone don't transform lives. Understanding people does.*

Over the past two decades, I've had the privilege of coaching people from every background: CEOs, entrepreneurs, couples, and parents. Again and again, the lesson is clear: when gender intelligence is applied, transformation accelerates.

I've watched marriages shift almost overnight when husbands stop fixing and start listening. I've seen female executives restore their energy and balance by replenishing oxytocin instead of relying on adrenaline. I've guided business owners to realize that presence with their family is just as valuable as financial provision, and once they rebalance, their marriages, their companies, and all their relationships flourish.

While there are countless coaching models available today, most focus on one or two dimensions, for example, business, mindset, or habits. Mars Venus Coaching is different because it integrates all four intelligences: physical, intellectual, emotional, and spiritual.

I've seen executives who've achieved record profits but feel like failures at home. I've seen women outwardly successful yet inwardly depleted. Mars Venus Coaching addresses the whole picture. It recognizes you can't separate personal life from professional success—they rise and fall together.

As we navigate our lives and relationships, it's important to frequently check in with ourselves and ask, *Am I growing in all four dimensions—physical, intellectual, emotional, and spiritual? Or am I neglecting one or more areas?*

> **Ultimately, balance is the foundation of lasting success, and holistic growth is the only sustainable growth.**

By understanding and applying the Mars Venus methodologies, I've witnessed marriages heal, leaders rise, parents reconnect, and individuals reclaim joy and purpose—all through the simple yet profound lens of gender intelligence.

Dr. John Gray's framework has changed millions of lives, including my own. For me, what began as a single coaching practice has grown into a seven-figure enterprise. Over the years, using my unique skill set, I've helped numerous individuals reshape their lives, create safe containers for their families, and step into the roles of the leaders, partners, and people they were meant to be. Additionally, the coaches I've trained to conduct this same work have spread the Mars Venus philosophy widely throughout their communities, multiplying its impact globally and making a genuine positive impact in the world.

When men and women master gender intelligence, they don't just survive; they flourish. And when they flourish, they elevate everyone around them. That ripple effect—from one life to another—is how we truly change the world.

> "At its core, gender intelligence is an active consciousness that views gender differences as strengths, not weaknesses. It's an understanding that both nature and nurture play a significant role in a person's life."
>
> **DR. JOHN GRAY**

TRUE TRANSFORMATION COMES FROM WITHIN

BEATRICE WÖLNER-HANSSEN &
STEFAN BURTH

Beatrice Wölner-Hanssen and Stefan Burth have been married for 20 years, are proud parents of three daughters, and passionate advocates for conscious relationships. Their shared journey as certified Mars Venus coaches has profoundly deepened their connection and transformed their approach to both love and life.

Beatrice holds a Master of Science in Architecture from ETH

Zurich and brings a rich, creative perspective to her work through her training in process-oriented art therapy. As a former professional volleyball player and avid world traveler, she blends structure and spontaneity in her coaching practice. Today, she works as a couples coach, integrating the Mars Venus philosophy into her sessions with individuals, couples, and groups. Her warm, grounded approach empowers clients to reconnect with themselves and each other in meaningful ways.

Stefan, who holds a Master of Economics from the University of St. Gallen, has built a successful career in banking. A committed family man and athlete, he brings heart, intellect, and clarity to all areas of life. While not a coach by profession, he serves as Beatrice's sparring partner, supporting her work with insight and curiosity. He also applies the Mars Venus principles in his professional environment, fostering better communication, understanding, and collaboration within teams.

Together, Beatrice and Stefan embody the principles of gender intelligence. Their commitment to growth, authenticity, and partnership shines through in their personal and professional lives. With humor, humility, and heartfelt presence, they inspire others to explore new dimensions of connection—within themselves, in their relationships, and beyond.

COACHING FROM LIVED EXPERIENCE

As a couple, we went through a very difficult time and were on the verge of separation. It felt like we had reached rock bottom—emotionally, physically, and in communication. But in that moment, we made a conscious decision: we would go the full journey together, no matter what it took. We didn't just want to save our relationship—we wanted to transform it into something truly extraordinary. That moment marked the beginning of a long and powerful journey.

Before discovering the Mars Venus philosophy, we engaged deeply with a wide range of relationship tools and methods. One of the central pillars of our learning journey was the Imago Dialogue method by Harville Hendrix, which we explored not only through his seminal book *Getting the Love You Want* but also by attending dedicated courses to deepen our understanding and practical application of the method. Beyond that, we integrated insights from attachment theory, somatic work, and conscious communication into both our personal relationship and our work with couples. Over the years, we studied many of the well-known classics in the field of relationship psychology, including *The 5 Love Languages* by Dr. Gary Chapman, *Hold Me Tight* by Dr. Sue Johnson, and *The Seven Principles for Making Marriage Work* by Dr. John Gottman.

Each of these resources gave us something valuable: language, insight, moments of clarity. They helped us better understand the emotional patterns shaped by our childhoods and the unconscious dynamics between us. They opened important doors.

Many of these approaches eventually led us back to our childhood histories. While those explorations were insightful, they often opened up broad, complex emotional landscapes that felt overwhelming. We would find ourselves stuck in deep introspection, without a clear way to move forward in the present. At times, it felt like we were excavating rather than rebuilding. We craved a path that was both emotionally meaningful and practically applicable in everyday life.

Looking back, all the methods we tried contributed to our relationship, each one adding something—insight, vocabulary, self-awareness. But nothing had a more lasting and practical impact than John Gray's Mars Venus philosophy. Why? Firstly, it's so easy to integrate into everyday life. Secondly, it's grounded in hormonal and neurological science—not just theory or opinion. Thirdly, it elevated our relationship to a completely new level. We found each other again with more depth, understanding, and connection than we ever thought possible.

The great strength of John Gray's work lies in two distinct qualities. Firstly, the profound insights he offers into the emotional and psychological dynamics between men and women. Secondly, the clarity and simplicity of his practical coaching system, which translates these insights into concrete, actionable steps for everyday life. Ultimately, it's this clarity and simplicity that make John Gray's approach so uniquely powerful and effective.

The Mars Venus philosophy didn't demand years of excavation or constant emotional processing. Instead, it gave us practical tools based on biological and neurological truths. We began to understand each other not just psychologically, but also hormonally. That made a huge difference. It felt accessible, respectful, and empowering. Gender intelligence allowed us to stop overanalyzing and start interacting differently—immediately and sustainably.

The more we explored the Mars Venus philosophy, the better we understood what it means to be a man or a woman in a relationship. For example, men are biologically single-focused. They don't thrive on multitasking or emotional complexity the way women often do, and, deep down, a man wants nothing more than to make his woman happy. Truly happy.

Another insight that had a profound effect was the idea that a man becomes a hero not by fixing or defending himself, but by learning to hold space for his partner's emotions—especially when they're intense or critical. When a woman expresses strong feelings—even if they come out sharp or personal—for a man, the ideal response is simply to breathe, listen, and reflect back what he heard. No defensiveness. No counterattack. Just presence. Once we understood gender intelligence, our relationship started to shift.

We also came to see how central oxytocin is for women—it's not a luxury, but a necessity. Learning that women are primarily responsible for creating the conditions for oxytocin to thrive within them was a game-changer. Often, a woman doesn't need to do more for her partner; she needs to receive more from him. She doesn't need to fix his problems; she needs to trust that he can handle them. For us, that shift—learning to lean back, soften, and listen—changed everything.

Even our sex life transformed. Not because we tried harder, but because our dynamic became more aligned with our biology and emotional wiring. When a woman no longer feels the pressure to be everything at once, it creates a shift in the bedroom. Finally, she feels seen, cherished, and allowed to simply be a woman

One tool that made a big difference was the Venus Talk. It's a simple ritual, but powerful: the man asks the woman how she's feeling—and just listens. No advice. No fixing. Just presence. That one act of emotional holding changed the tone of our conversations, our daily evening walks, our weekends. It gives the woman space to feel and be without needing to perform. Overall, we began to understand ourselves better and, in turn, began to see each other more clearly. Everything became more relaxed. Even conflicts didn't feel as dramatic anymore—because we both recognized more quickly that many of our tensions weren't personal, but biological. It wasn't about who was right or wrong. It was about learning to dance with our differences.

And yet, we want to be clear: this isn't magic. It's a daily practice. We still fall into old patterns from time to time. We still need reminders. But the difference is—we now know how to get back on track. We have a shared language. A shared philosophy. And we have the willingness to keep showing up for each other. That, to us, is real love. And we're so grateful for it.

After repairing and enhancing our own relationship, becoming certified Mars Venus coaches was the natural next step. We wanted to share with others what had helped us so much, as individuals, as a couple, and as a family. Today, we bring this wisdom into our work with clients, groups, and teams—and into our own lives, every single day.

Our clients often tell us they feel seen and understood in ways they haven't felt before. They sense that we're not just offering tools—we're offering truth, empathy, and real-world tools. That's a powerful connection. We've walked this path ourselves. We've faced the challenges, made the mistakes, had the fights, and rebuilt the trust—*together*. We don't coach from a theoretical distance; we coach from lived experience.

STRENGTH COMES FROM UNDERSTANDING

Of course, coaching comes with challenges. Some clients come in with deep wounds, resistance, or very little hope. Others expect instant results without effort. Our job is to hold the space for them, walk alongside them, and—sometimes—challenge them lovingly.

We also recognize that each individual and couple must take responsibility for their own path. We can provide tools, insights, and encouragement, but the real work must come from within. And that's where true transformation begins.

One couple came to us feeling more like roommates than lovers. Their relationship had become transactional. The spark was gone. Communication was mechanical, and emotional intimacy had faded. Through Mars Venus coaching, we guided them in rediscovering their masculine and feminine energies. They learned to meet each other's core needs again and speak in ways that would actually be heard. With simple tools and deeper understanding, they slowly rekindled connection. Today, they laugh together, hold hands again, and are rediscovering passion and emotional closeness—on a level they hadn't experienced in years.

Love isn't a straight line. Real relationships go through highs and lows. The secret isn't to avoid conflict, but to understand it. To face it. To grow through it and let it make you stronger than you've ever been.

Another powerful transformation happened with a woman who came to us feeling lost. On the surface, she was incredibly successful—driven, high-achieving, and on track for even more accomplishments in a male-dominated business world. But inside, she felt disconnected. The spark and joy that once lit up her life had all but disappeared.

As we explored her story, it became clear that she had unintentionally disconnected from her feminine energy. Her life lacked oxytocin-producing activities—the ones that nourish, replenish, and allow women to feel truly alive. Once we introduced her to the Mars Venus philosophy, particularly the understanding that she was responsible for 90 percent of her own happiness, things began to shift dramatically. She made a personal list of everything that could raise her oxytocin levels—even small moments like watching a sunset or waiting at the bus stop became intentional opportunities for joy. Week by week, her energy changed. Within a few short weeks, she had transformed. Her zest for life returned, and she was ready to face challenges that had once overwhelmed her. Witnessing her step fully into her feminine power—and seeing how inspired she became by seeing what healthy femininity looked like—was one of the most fulfilling parts of our journey as coaches.

And this transformation isn't limited to women. We've seen men change just as powerfully.

When men experience what real, grounded feminine energy feels like, it awakens something in them. They begin to value women on a deeper level and naturally step into their masculine roles as providers and protectors. We've seen men who had struggled for years with infidelity suddenly commit to loyalty. We've watched broken men, devastated by past relationships, find the strength to open their hearts again.

It's an honor to witness these shifts—when both men and women reclaim their true essence. Because when they do, everything changes: love, relationships, careers, and even self-worth.

EQUALITY DOESN'T EQUAL SAMENESS

Equality between men and women is a core value for us. It's one of the great achievements of our time. But equality doesn't mean sameness. Yes, we're all unique individuals shaped by upbringing, culture, and life experience, but biologically, hormonally, neurologically, we're different. We think differently, make decisions differently, and process emotions differently. These differences affect the way we communicate, cope with stress, and connect emotionally. Understanding this has been nothing short of transformative for us and our clients.

When we learn how testosterone, estrogen, and oxytocin influence our behaviors—how men often need to "cave" to rebuild testosterone, or how women need to feel seen, heard, and supported to restore oxytocin—we stop taking things personally. We start creating space for mutual understanding instead of blame.

Gender intelligence opened our eyes—and hearts. It has helped us thrive not only as a couple, but also as parents, coworkers, and leaders. It allows us to see each other more clearly and relate more compassionately.

One of the most touching validations of this came from our children. Our three daughters lived through our toughest times as a couple. Years later, they each told us how much gender intelligence has changed our relationship and their lives. They said they want to model their future relationships on ours—but not because we're perfect. It's not about perfection. It's about presence. It's about showing up again and again, even when it's hard. *Especially* when it's hard. As a couple, we're real, and we're constantly growing. In addition, our children understand the boys their age so much better now, and it's made their lives—and relationships—richer and more harmonious. That compliment from the three young, honest human beings who witness us every day reminded us how deeply this work matters—not just for couples, but for future generations too.

OUR MESSAGE

If there's one message we want to convey, it's this: We've been through the darkness. We know how painful it can be when a relationship feels lost. We also know how beautiful, playful, and fulfilling it can become—with the right tools, deep commitment, and emotional honesty.

> **Today, we're living the best relationship we've ever had—with more love, more connection, and yes, better sex than ever before. But the road to get here wasn't easy.**

It was messy, nonlinear, and full of effort. We had to face ourselves and each other, again and again—but it was absolutely worth it.

And that's the heart of our work. We don't promise shortcuts. We offer support, guidance, and a proven philosophy. We walk with people through the hard parts—especially when others give up.

In fact, we have a bit of a motto: *when others stop, we begin.*

> "Our differences aren't mistakes—they're meaningful. When we understand and adapt to these differences with empathy and skill, relationships flourish instead of fail."
>
> **DR. JOHN GRAY**

THE SUPERPOWER OF GENDER INTELLIGENCE

MARISA YNEZ

Marisa Ynez is a master guide in feminine embodiment and sacred sexuality with over two decades of coaching experience. Her path began through early life challenges that awakened innate gifts of deep intuitive understanding and the capacity to help others heal. By her 20s, she was already mentoring successful female entrepreneurs.

In the years that followed, her work evolved as she incorporated the body-based wisdom of her practice with elements of nonerotic meditation, somatic awareness, sound healing, and quantum insight—each becoming a vital thread in transformation.

Now as a certified Mars Venus gender intelligence coach, personally trained by renowned relationship expert John Gray, Marisa blends science and spirit in a grounded, heart-centered methodology, distinguished by her profound understanding of the wisdom of yoni—Sanskrit for womb, origin, the totality of the female sexual and reproductive systems. She meets you on your current level of growth and lovingly guides you beyond who you've been in the past.

Marisa's clients include visionary and spiritual women and men, and purpose-driven couples who value deep connection and partnership. She demystifies the female prostate, empowers the wisdom of the yoni, and teaches women and men how to reset not just their nervous systems, but their entire way of being. With this embodied recalibration, they step into a more vibrant and empowered expression of how they love, lead, express, and live.

GENDER INTELLIGENCE—THE KEY TO EXPONENTIAL UNDERSTANDING

For me, gender intelligence began with my own personal experiences. I'm an expert at being female, an advocate for women and monogamous couples, and a childhood sexual abuse survivor turned thriver. Feminine healing is the foundation of my flourishing life and business.

> **When a woman heals her wounded feminine, especially after sexual trauma, her life gets easier, and she can establish loving relationships with less effort.**

The inspiration to be a Mars Venus gender intelligence coach grew as I embodied so much life-changing and exciting material learned from John Gray. His vast knowledge and experience continue to benefit me, my romantic and platonic relationships, and especially impact my clients through my Messages from Yoni transformation program.

Feminine and masculine energy are essential components of my work, which includes nonerotic guided yoni meditations, feminine embodiment practices, and a foundational study of the female prostate and ejaculation. During my coaching sessions, I often catch myself telling clients, "John Gray says …"

In the last 20 years, I've seen far more women desiring (and needing) honest communication in their relationships, fulfilling sexual skills, and intimacy with their partners. Committing to self-improvement and healing is key to building a healthy relationship with someone who's right for you. It's important to know that just because you love someone, it doesn't mean they're your ideal partner. However, doing the work gives us the knowledge, wisdom, and tools to determine who *is* right for us and strengthen all the important relationships in our lives.

Women are increasingly on their masculine side as they manage overwhelming lives—heading households, providing their own protection and security, making major decisions independently, lacking the assistance of a partner. This emphasizes the necessity of cultivating and nurturing healthy inner femininity daily.

Using her power can alter a woman's world in miraculous ways, positively affecting her experience of self, the men she dates, the way she lives, the man she marries, the babies she creates, as well as the impact on her community, family, and friends. That's why gender intelligence is so valuable—it not only helps us better understand the other gender but also ourselves.

Feminine and Masculine Energy Attributes

FEMININE ENERGY	MASCULINE ENERGY
Love and Expansion	Purpose and Focus
Receptivity and Flow	Action and Direction
Beauty and Creativity	Strength and Production
Openness and Vulnerability	Protection and Stability
Beingness	Doingness
Cyclical	Linear
Intuitive	Logical
Emotional	Rational
Connection-Oriented	Goal-Oriented
Communication and Relationship	Problem-Solving and Achievement
Caring and Harmony	Providing and Order
Collaborative	Competitive
Expresses Needs and Desires	Fulfills Needs and Pursues Challenges

Perceiving and understanding one's masculine and feminine polarity is a superpower—and the perception and understanding of your opposite gender is *exponential* power.

THE SPARK THAT LIT THE PATH TO HEALING

In my late teens and young adult years, my consciousness expanded. Although I had a deep longing for friends and a relationship, my unwanted behavior pushed them away. I had no idea my actions were symptoms of trauma. The way I acted and the things I said weren't the real me. Deep down, I was desperate and willing to try anything to change, to get better, to *feel* better. In trying to cope with my trauma, I experienced waves of promiscuity and then prudishness and loneliness, and I cheated on partners, sabotaged growth opportunities, lied to my parents, often didn't keep my word, overate, drank and took drugs, became addicted to pornography, skipped classes, and had two abortions. Suffice to say, the list of coping methods abuse victims can adopt is long. Why was I being like this? Was this my life forever? I prayed to God to show me a better way and take away the emotional pain and hopelessness.

I vividly remember the moment, during a perfect California summer evening, that activated my healing journey. Excited about my new role as a live-in nanny, I drove to my mom's house for the last of my belongings. One second, I was driving, watching the sunset; the next was a moment unlike any I'd experienced before—or any I've experienced since. I saw a close-up view of a vintage slide deck projecting images of all the instances of my abuse in rapid succession.

Almost like watching a movie, I saw myself at 15, the summer my dad almost caught a guy in my bedroom past midnight. I had never told anyone that Travis, the 25-year-old down the street, had been sneaking into my room for almost a year, since a month after I turned 14. Initially, he'd often drive by and start a conversation with me; then he moved on to walking in front of my house. When we were alone, he introduced me to pornographic magazines. By the start of freshman year, he was incessantly knocking on my bedroom window almost every school night until I opened it.

Travis called me his girlfriend and said once I turned 18, we'd get married. This thought made me as ill as his visits, yet being so young, I believed he meant to marry me. What he did to me during his visits made me nauseated and physically exhausted, but I couldn't stop because I didn't know how to say no. Praying, wishing, hoping, hating every second of it didn't make it end. In my child's mind, I felt like I was to blame, a common side effect for abuse victims. I was afraid to tell on him for fear of getting into trouble. Guilt and shame gnawed at me, and I felt forced to endure the abuse, with no end in sight.

As I drove to my mom's house, the flashbacks continued, leaving me dazed. My breath became shallow as I recounted the emotional impact of each relived memory and recognized how many intensely awful things I had blocked from my past. Thankfully, the abuse came to an end when my father found out while my mother was out of town with family.

Around midnight, my youngest sister was unusually fussy, so my dad took her on a walk. As Dad strolled up the street toward the mountain foothills, he passed the front of our house and glanced down the side of the property. He made a mental note of the screen having fallen off my window and would replace it when he returned home.

After he settled my sister in bed, he went out back to the side of the house. The window was open and the shade down. He heard two distinct voices, one mine and one male. Maybe his subconscious fatherly self-preservation led him to not want to see his daughter and what she could possibly be doing with a boy in her room. So instead of pushing the shade aside to find out who was in my room, my dad ran back into the house and violently banged on my locked bedroom door.

Wearing only socks, Travis darted to the window and jumped out, and I threw his clothes and shoes in a secret space between my headboard and bed. Nude myself, I threw a robe on and slowly walked to the door, giving him ample time to hide outside.

After I opened the door, my dad charged into the room like a rabid animal, screaming, "Where is he? Where the f*** is he?" I'd never heard my dad swear before or become that angry. He searched any place a person could hide, checking under the bed and throwing every cabinet door open. He shoved aside jackets and dresses in my closet.

Satisfied the room was clear, he ran out to the front door and back outside to try and catch whoever had been in my room. I closed my door and collapsed against it. To my surprise, instead of crying, panicking, or worrying about being in trouble, the biggest, uncontrollable smile spread across my face—I was so relieved and happy. My dad saved me.

With nothing but socks on, Travis had crouched down at the bottom of our huge backyard slope in the cold, with lots of slugs, underneath the peach tree surrounded by tall overgrowth. After about five hours, the sun started to rise, and he returned for his clothes. I quickly shoved his belongings out the window, and he took off fast. Travis never tapped on my window again.

I was grounded for the rest of the summer until school started in late September. It was the best punishment I ever had. I was safe, nurtured, and, although dysfunctional, able to be a teenager again.

Then other terrible memories popped onto the ethereal screen before me. At 15, my grandpa first abused me; then it happened again at 19 years old, when I was standing alone with him in his living room. After asking him for a small loan to help fix my car, my grandpa handed me a check, and I hugged him in thanks, but the embrace turned into a nightmarish event. My grandpa started sucking on my ear and neck, groping me. Horrified, I froze in place, unable to respond to the visceral experience. When I finally came to my senses, I pulled back from the most vile and sickening hold. He looked into my eyes and said, "I'm sorry. I hope that was

OK. I just couldn't help myself."

During the drive, more images presented themselves, and the unsettling feelings seemed to last forever. Then, *poof!* Startled and shaken, I snapped back into consciousness. I was parked in my mom's driveway. I shut off the engine, with no idea how I had driven home over the last 15 minutes. I hadn't been present to the road or traffic and thanked my subconscious mind for seeing me safely home.

I couldn't unknow what was revealed to me in the car, and like a bad smell, it followed me everywhere. Shortly thereafter, like magic, as if the Universe responded to a prayer, I acquired John's book, *What You Feel, You Can Heal.* I knew I needed to surrender to the fire of this work. His simple yet profound approach was the catalyst for genuine and honest communication between myself and my family that didn't exist before and continues to this day.

I attribute my first significant rise in courage to John's "Love Letter" technique, which I used on myself. The premise of this healing method is: You write a letter in five parts to someone, each with prompts that lead you through a series of emotions. It begins with expressing anger and blame, then moving through different levels, including hurt and sadness, fear and insecurity, guilt and responsibility, until you get to love. The purpose is to release all unhealthy feelings that stop us from experiencing and sharing love with ourselves and others.[10]

Here's a brief example of my love letter to myself, with John Gray's prompts in italics:

I don't like it when I don't take care of myself and I dress like a guy. *I resent* my depression. *I hate it when* I don't brush my hair. *I'm fed up with* making myself ugly. *I'm tired of* having people staring like they feel sorry for me. *I want to* feel beautiful.

I feel sad when I hurt the people I love. *I feel hurt because* I keep making decisions that get me into trouble. *I feel awful because* my parents are worried. *I feel disappointed because* I want to be and do better, and I don't know how. *I want to know* what it feels like to feel good and normal.

I feel afraid of death all the time. *I'm afraid that* I'll never be successful. *I feel scared because* I'm hanging around the wrong people. *I want to start* focusing on my music.

I'm sorry that I'm not a better daughter and human. *I'm sorry for* lying. *Please forgive me for* having two abortions. *I didn't mean to* be so careless with my body. *I wish* I knew how beautiful I am.

I love myself because I'm doing my best. *I love when* I take care of myself. *I understand that* I'm scared. *I forgive myself for* not knowing how to tell Travis and my grandpa no and to stop. *I want to* heal and feel happy in my body and life.

—Love, Marisa

This healing modality helped me get clear on my feelings and what I wanted, then served as practice for writing and verbally expressing my emotions. Although I needed to employ the Love Letter technique numerous times over many months, both for Travis and my grandfather, I did so until the stories—thoughts of and feelings about the incidents—lost their energetic charge. With the practice of processing my feminine emotions and getting clear on the masculine direction I was headed, my self-confidence grew. Despite the fact it took almost a year after the flashbacks to finally verbalize my darkest, scariest secrets to my mom and eventually my dad, I developed trust in my relationship with them. Over time, as the heavy weight of the secret lifted, I attracted healthier relationships, broke a pattern of silence, and gained my joyful freedom.

FINDING MY VOICE, CONFRONTING MY ABUSER

Later that year, while attending a transformation retreat, I decided to call my grandpa and hold him accountable for his abuse, confronting him from my masculine and honoring my feminine need for safety of distance. I used a pay phone at the event hotel because my cell phone had died. First, my beloved Nana answered the phone. She was surprised, as I had never called my grandpa before, and she seemed suspicious about why I wanted to speak to him and not her. An awkward energy rose between us until she put my grandpa on the line.

His voice boomed into my ear, and I spoke before I changed my mind. "Grandpa, I remember what you did to me. I remember everything." I then described each incident, careful not to speak in a way that sounded salacious so he didn't get any gratification from my telling. I wanted him to know I remembered every detail of what he did to me and for him to take responsibility for all of his actions.

When my grandpa physically violated me, my body acted as if under a spell, and shock didn't allow me to respond to him the way I had wanted. After the flashback of him giving me the loan, I frequently berated myself for reacting in freeze mode and then running off without confronting him.

I said, "I remember telling you it was OK. I looked you in the eye, nodded my head, and whispered, 'Yes, it's fine.' But it wasn't fine. What you did to me was not OK. You broke my trust. I looked up to you. I feel so betrayed by you. You knew I didn't grow up with my biological father. You and my dad became the men I looked up to, and you broke that bond with me forever."

After I finished speaking, he was quiet for so long that I had to add a few quarters to the pay phone. It took every ounce of my willpower to not interrupt the silence but rather let it hang, for him to feel exposed and not off the hook. Swelling with pride and courage, I deeply inhaled and exhaled, holding steadfast to the reins of my power, feeling fully connected to my truth. My fierce masculine boldness spoke for me as I laid down a boundary.

"From this moment on," I said, "you are never allowed to hug or touch me again. I will not stay away from Nana, so that means at any family gatherings, we will not be interacting anymore. In the future, when I have children, you are never allowed to touch or hold them. Do you understand?"

"Yes," he mumbled. "I'm so sorry. I didn't mean to." The moment grew heavy again with more deafening silence. That was all he had for me? Was this vapid apology enough? Right then, an intuitive message reminded me I didn't call to hear his words. I was confronting my abuser head-on to self-advocate. I called him to use my voice, which had eluded me when he fondled me.

After a long pause, with nothing more to say, I firmly said, "Goodbye" and hung up in slow motion, hyperaware of how finalizing that moment felt. It was a goodbye to epigenetic victim energy, silence, self-loathing. Never again did I have to feel obligated to politely hug him hello and feel disloyal to my body as it screamed to not let him touch me. It was done.

Wobbly kneed, my eyes ruptured into tears, and I stabilized myself on a dusty wall. I felt elated, as a past deceit and suffering shifted into truthful courage and empowerment. A sense of being more my truest self washed over me. My commitment to speaking up paid off. I resolved the energetic entanglement, and my newfound voice led me into a powerful sense of womanhood and life purpose.

AUTHENTIC FEMININE ENERGY RECLAIMED

John's modeling and encouragement of honest communication regarding sensitive subjects like love, sex, money, marriage, children, death, gender, and many other significant areas gave me permission to voice my own truths about sexual abuse and develop my femininity, despite the dysfunctional masculine energy keeping me in fear as a child and young woman.

Coming out of the trauma fog, I was aware I had been angry at my parents for not keeping me safe. I was furious at all the males, especially those who had hurt me physically and emotionally, labeling men as nasty and only wanting one thing. This belief was in contrast with my inherent desire for true love and a future family of my own. Still, I swung to my broken male side out of protection, being tough and independent when going out, chasing men, sleeping with them too fast. Like other abuse victims, I craved sex because making it my decision gave me a false sense of control. Insomnia developed from overwhelm and constant vigilance, not feeling safe in my home and never out in public.

It's important for women to develop their feminine side and create homeostasis with their masculine energy. Beginning by diligently focusing on healing myself, then following the masculine-feminine wisdom around healthy relationships devised by John Gray, I've been able to generate compounding physical and emotional rewards. With will and practice, this process led to the next layer of development in restoring my mind and body health.

I began recognizing when I was acting needy and insecure and became aware of when my emotions grew out of proportion. I had been expressing a fraction of my feelings, not the full truth, which John refers to as the "iceberg effect." I also identified what John calls the "seesaw effect," the suppression and resistance of my emotions, which can cause a rise of emotions in others around me as they mirror what I'm feeling.[11]

Incrementally, I learned to transform unhealthy behaviors or beliefs into things that served me, through journaling, meditation, yoga, mantras, sound baths, reiki, traditional therapy, acupuncture, breath work, workshops, and retreats. I also advanced to a stage where I was ready and willing to study sacred sexuality with myself and my partner.

With practical application, I restored and reclaimed my authentic feminine energy—feeling and expressing my emotions, allowing myself to feel beautiful and attractive, appreciating men, being openhearted and loving, and developing my intuition. With my partner, I became softer and vulnerable while we communicated or made love. All the while, I appropriately leveraged masculine energy when I needed to take charge and lead in business, plan outcomes, be assertive, set boundaries, problem solve, or teach others through my specialized programs.

By understanding my female gender and how to access and use my feminine energy, I gained awareness of the energetic toggling between each polarity. This isn't to be thought of as a 50-50 exchange, but rather a ratio that flows between either polarity, resting at will in one more than the other, depending on what life requires of me at the time. I've internalized John Gray's philosophy and his thorough familiarity with the distinguishing characteristics between men and women, the way they communicate, behave, and interact with each other.

Gender intelligence is being aware of the differences between men and women, resulting in more love-filled relationships, profound physical intimacy, raising better children, and experiencing a more cohesive workplace and society.

This, I feel, is the ultimate goal of John Gray's teachings and the foundation of my own work at Messages from Yoni.

> "True healing happens when we give space for our deepest emotions. The 'Love Letter' is one of the most powerful tools I've ever taught to help men and women reconnect with themselves and each other."
>
> **DR. JOHN GRAY**

MARS VENUS IN INDIA

Love Beyond Expectations

KAWAL ARORA

Kawal Arora is a seasoned Mars Venus relationship coach in India with over a decade of experience helping individuals, couples, parents, teens, working professionals, leaders, heads of departments, and start-up founders navigate the complexities of relationships. With a deep understanding of human emotions and relationship dynamics, Kawal has worked with hundreds of people, empowering them to build stronger, more fulfilling connections. His coaching focuses on helping individuals break unhealthy relationship patterns and cultivate meaningful bonds based on understanding, trust, and love. His corporate coaching helps leaders and teams overcome gender-based workplace challenges, leading to better teamwork, reduced conflicts, and improved productivity.

Kawal also conducts seminars and workshops in organizations, equipping professionals with the skills and awareness needed to build healthy workplace relationships, effective communication, and strong leadership.

His work bridges the gap between traditional relationship wisdom and modern psychological insights, offering a fresh perspective on how to build lasting, fulfilling relationships in today's world.

GENDER INTELLIGENCE—AN EFFECTIVE AND VERSATILE TOOL

We are never taught how to navigate relationships—especially marriage. By default, we tend to conduct ourselves in relationships based on how we saw our parents behave in theirs. We unconsciously absorb our understanding of what to do or not to do from those early observations. However, this often doesn't work because the dynamics are entirely different. The individuals are different; the environment has changed; the time and societal context are no longer the same, and, most importantly, the emotional needs of partners today are vastly different. Without updated awareness and guidance, this inherited approach can lead to confusion, conflict, and disconnection.

After marriage, a husband often struggles to balance the expectations of his wife and parents, without knowing how to handle conflicts. When he sides with his parents without analyzing the situation, his wife loses trust, and she doesn't feel safe—a woman's primary need in a relationship—which can deeply affect her emotional well-being. This struggle exists in both love and arranged marriages.

On the other hand, a wife also needs to make her husband feel wanted and needed, which is a man's primary need in a relationship. He needs to be acknowledged and appreciated for his efforts. Unfortunately, most couples don't realize how small actions and misunderstandings build up over time, leading to emotional disconnect. Lack of knowledge about the role of hormones during stressful situations makes things worse.

In my coaching, I emphasize that both partners don't have to attend coaching together. Even if just one person seeks guidance, it reduces stress, provides clarity, and brings awareness about their partner's expectations. Many of my clients have experienced significant positive changes in their relationships simply by understanding how to conduct themselves differently.

Although gender intelligence helps couples and individuals improve their current relationships, I strongly advocate for learning gender intelligence early—before entering a relationship. Couples in a relationship, soon to be married, or newlyweds can benefit greatly from this knowledge. When you understand how men and women function differently in relationships, you naturally create harmony, love, and happiness for yourself and your partner.

By default, we tend to believe that others—regardless of their gender—should think, feel, and react the same way we do in a given situation. This assumption leads to misunderstandings, frustration, and conflicts, especially in personal and professional relationships. We expect others to approach problems, make decisions, and communicate in ways that feel natural to us, without realizing that men and women often perceive, process, and express themselves differently. This lack of awareness creates unnecessary friction, not because people are wrong, but because they are different.

Beyond personal relationships, gender intelligence is equally important in the workplace. Businesses thrive not just on strategies and numbers but also on relationships and trust. Whether you're dealing with clients, employees, or partners, the key is understanding people. Applying gender intelligence in business helps create stronger teams, better communication, and fewer conflicts, ultimately leading to growth and success.

Organizations should prioritize educating their employees on fostering effective collaboration and communication between genders. Through the regular sessions I conduct in organizations, I often receive feedback that this knowledge is eye-opening and not available elsewhere. Employees realize its impact not just in their professional lives but also in their personal lives—especially parents who now better understand their children, particularly teenagers.

Although I have many examples—both my own and from my clients—where gender intelligence has brought remarkable transformation, I'll share an experience from my professional life that truly cemented its importance for me.

As an IT professional, I once transitioned into a new role and inherited an existing team. They were skilled and competent, but like any team, they faced challenges—frequent arguments, differences of opinion, and conflicts over expectations. When I took the time to listen to them individually, a common theme emerged: there was a noticeable gap in male and female team members' perceptions, understandings, and expectations of one another. Some even described it as gender bias in the workplace. These unspoken, unmet expectations were causing friction, making collaboration difficult.

Being a Mars Venus Coach, I quickly recognized that this was not about bias but about a lack of gender intelligence. People weren't intentionally creating conflict; they simply didn't understand the different ways in which men and women communicate, make decisions, and respond to challenges.

To address this, I coached individual team members, helping them see the other gender's perspective. For female team members, I realized that simply listening to their concerns without immediately trying to "fix" things made a significant difference.

Women often feel safe and valued when their thoughts and challenges are acknowledged, so instead of offering instant solutions, I spent more time actively listening. This made them feel heard and more open to discussions.

For male team members, I helped them understand where their female colleagues were coming from, explaining why certain reactions or concerns were valid. I also encouraged and appreciated their efforts when they made even small adjustments in how they interacted with their female teammates. Surprisingly, when the men made these small shifts, the women naturally reciprocated, adjusting their own ways of working. The conflicts that once seemed like deadlocks eased, making way for a healthier, more collaborative team dynamic.

All of this was possible simply by applying gender intelligence and basic Mars Venus concepts at work. This experience reinforced my belief that gender intelligence isn't just important in personal relationships but is crucial in the professional world as well. It can help teams function better, reduce misunderstandings, and create a work environment where men and women complement each other's strengths rather than struggle against their differences.

I highly recommend that all professionals—especially leaders and managers—develop gender intelligence. Organizations should actively educate their employees on how to effectively collaborate with team members of different genders. It can be a game changer in solving many people-related challenges and building harmonious, high-performing teams.

By applying gender intelligence, you can:
- Build stronger teams in business and corporations by recognizing how men and women communicate and work differently.
- Create deeper relationships by understanding how your team members' emotional needs differ.
- Improve coaching and leadership by adapting your communication style to the other person's needs.

At the end of the day, success isn't about how much you do but how well you connect with people. When you understand what the other person needs to feel connected, you unlock the power to build meaningful relationships, strong businesses, and a fulfilling life.

MY MARS VENUS REVELATION

Gender intelligence wasn't a tool I added to my coaching tool kit until later in my career. I was already working as an ICF certified professional life coach, formally helping people navigate their personal and professional challenges, when I discovered the Mars Venus methodology.

As a life coach, I noticed a recurring theme: most of the issues people brought to me were related to relationships. Most women's complaints related to not feeling safe and loved, trust issues, and being the only giver in the relationship. On the other hand, men complained about giving their lives to the relationship, not being able to understand their partners, always finding their partners complaining, and feeling that nothing they did was ever enough. While I helped them to the best of my ability, I often found myself questioning, *Why are so many people struggling with the same kinds of relationship challenges?* I knew there had to be a deeper, underlying reason, so I began searching for answers.

I believe the seeds of my journey to become a Mars Venus relationship coach were planted early in life. Growing up, I found myself in a unique position: my cousins, friends, and schoolmates would often confide in me, sharing their stories and struggles, not necessarily about relationships but about various aspects of life. I became the keeper of many secrets, a role that continued into my college years and even in my professional life. This made me wonder: *why did people share their challenges with me so openly, without hesitation?* My curiosity led me to ask a few of them why they chose me as their confidant. Their answers were surprisingly consistent: they found it easy to talk to me because I listened without judgment. That realization was a turning point. I understood I had a natural ability—the power of listening without judgment.

At first, I leaned into this strength and started intently listening to people. It helped them feel heard and understood, but I felt there had to be something more I could do beyond just listening. That's when I discovered coaching, recognizing its potential to create real change. When I discovered Mars Venus, it was a revelation. Understanding why men and women behave differently, how they communicate, and what they need in a relationship gave me the clarity I was looking for.

It was eye-opening to realize that many relationship struggles come not from a lack of love but from a lack of understanding of the opposite gender.

When I started bringing this awareness to individuals and couples, I saw remarkable transformations. When people begin to understand their partners instead of expecting them to think, feel, or react the same way they do, conflicts dissolve, and connections strengthen.

Research in neuroscience and psychology shows that humans are wired for connection. The brain releases oxytocin, often called the "bonding hormone," when we feel heard, understood, and valued. This applies in personal and professional life. Whether you're leading a team, running a business, coaching someone, or nurturing a relationship, the key to influence and impact is making the other person feel connected, safe, and valued.

My understanding of gender intelligence has made my work incredibly fulfilling. Helping people bridge the gap between their expectations and their partner's reality has not only saved relationships but also helped individuals find joy and harmony in their personal lives. Mars Venus Coaching isn't just about fixing relationships—it's about making them thrive.

MARS VENUS METHODOLOGY IN ACTION

In India, love is often seen as sacrifice and compromise. But true love is understanding and support. The more you understand your partner's needs, fears, and desires, the deeper your connection will be. Love isn't about changing each other—it's about growing together.

As a leading relationship coach in India, I've contextualized Dr. John Gray's Mars Venus concepts to the unique cultural fabric of Indian society. Unlike in the West, Indian marriages aren't just a union of two individuals but an intricate web of relationships involving families on both sides. The expectations, traditions, and social pressures make marital relationships one of the most complex in the world. In the absence of the right knowledge, people often find themselves struggling in their relationships, feeling overwhelmed by the need to manage expectations—of each other, their families, extended families, and even society. In the process, they gradually lose sight of the love, the basic ingredient of a successful relationship. Instead of experiencing the joy of partnership, they become entangled in fulfilling duties and obligations, missing out on the beauty of two souls uniting. Many couples, despite their best efforts, feel emotionally disconnected, leading to dissatisfaction, conflicts, and even separation.

One client, Ajay (name changed), first reached out to me in the middle of the night, desperate for help. He and his wife Garima (name changed) were living in the U.S. and had known each other for over a decade before marriage, yet their relationship had become dysfunctional a few months after tying the knot. Their struggles weren't just between them but were deeply entangled with family expectations—a common challenge for Indian couples, especially when living abroad while their families remain in India.

When Ajay shared their story, he spoke about their frequent arguments, misunderstandings, and how their marriage had become emotionally exhausting. He was overwhelmed, unable to figure out why knowing each other for years didn't translate into a smoother marriage. As I listened, I could immediately sense the unspoken emotions behind their struggles. I explained to Ajay what Garima was likely experiencing emotionally, the unmet expectations she carried, and why she often reacted the way she did. Ajay was shocked. He couldn't believe how accurately I had described Garima's feelings—without even talking to her—on our very first call, which he'd only made to enquire about coaching. He admitted that she had often expressed similar concerns, but he had never truly understood the "why" behind them.

Before coming to me, they had tried multiple marriage counselors, but none had helped Ajay understand the underlying emotional needs of their relationship. My coaching gave him that clarity. They embarked on a transformational journey, shifting their focus from blame to understanding.

Within a few months, their frequent fights lessened, and they started appreciating each other's perspectives. Garima, who had once felt trapped under the weight of expectations from both Ajay and her in-laws, even having suicidal thoughts, started reclaiming her individuality by focusing on herself. She enrolled in baking and dance classes, rediscovering her childhood passions, and upskilled herself to reenter the job market. Ajay, who had been constantly stressed managing situations between Garima and his parents, found a new sense of focus in his career and business.

Their story is a testament to how understanding gender differences and emotional needs can transform relationships. Sometimes, it's not about fixing a partner but about understanding them better. Love needs understanding, communication, and the right expectations to thrive. When couples understand each other's emotional needs, their bonds strengthen effortlessly.

LOVE ALONE IS NOT ENOUGH

When I first met Sujoy and Divya (names changed), they had been married for 14 years and appeared to be the perfect couple. They shared a deep bond built on love, understanding, and mutual respect. From the outside, their relationship looked strong and inspiring, something many others admired. They had even set clear relationship rules for themselves—like prioritizing quality time together, going on regular dates, making space for open conversations, and ensuring that both partners contributed equally to keeping the spark alive. They had no major typical in-laws-related issues and were often seen as role models for other couples who sought their guidance. Yet, beneath this seemingly flawless relationship, something was amiss. Their arguments were increasing in frequency, and both were feeling emotionally drained. Their mental well-being was taking a hit, and they couldn't understand why. How could a couple that had done everything "right" still struggle in their relationship?

The truth is, even with the right intentions and immense love, relationships can face challenges due to a lack of gender intelligence. As I worked with them, I peeled back the layers of their relationship. While everything seemed perfect on the surface, I discovered that they had spoken and unspoken expectations—some realistic and others unrealistic, sometimes expressed and other times not. More importantly, they didn't know how to react when those expectations weren't met. When facing challenges, they were functioning as two well-intentioned individuals rather than one unified team.

Over the next few weeks, through coaching, we explored their past and discovered that the life they had been living for years had been shaping their views, actions, and decisions in the present. Finally, they started to understand why the other person behaved in certain ways. This awareness transformed how they responded to each other. Instead of reacting emotionally, they made small but meaningful adjustments in their thought patterns and behaviors. These subtle shifts created profound changes, bringing them back to the loving and harmonious relationship they'd always had—but now with an even deeper connection and newfound wisdom.

> **Sometimes, even the strongest relationships need fine-tuning. When love is combined with the right awareness, a good relationship can evolve into an extraordinary one.**

One of the biggest challenges in India when it comes to relationships isn't just the lack of awareness between partners but also the lack of awareness that help is available. Most people don't even realize relationship coaching exists. They assume their struggles—whether marital conflicts, family pressure, or emotional disconnect—are just part of life and must be endured rather than addressed. Many couples suffer in silence, believing that seeking help means admitting failure. Unlike in the West, where therapy and coaching are more commonly accepted, in India relationship challenges are often brushed under the carpet or left to be solved by family elders who, unfortunately, may not always have the right tools to guide them.

Many people in India confuse coaching with advice-giving. But coaching isn't about telling someone what to do; it's about helping them discover their own answers. A great coach asks the right questions, brings awareness, and empowers people to make better choices. Most couples who have gone through remarkable transformations via coaching hesitate to share their success stories with others. If they did, it would help others come forward and get the help they need.

In Indian culture and cultures that have close-knit family ties, life is deeply connected with family, friendships, and societal expectations. But true fulfillment comes when you learn to balance external responsibilities with internal peace. The happiest people aren't those who have everything, but those who have meaningful relationships.

> "Gender intelligence is just as critical in the boardroom as it is in the bedroom. When we apply these principles to workplace dynamics, communication improves, stress goes down, and collaboration goes up."
>
> **DR. JOHN GRAY**

UNLOCK EXCLUSIVE BONUS CONTENT!

Dr. John Gray and his certified coaches have created powerful resources to enhance your understanding of gender intelligence and the wider Mars Venus philosophy.

Inside your free bonus pack, you'll get:
- Audio downloads
- Printable worksheets
- Practical tools and resources—and more!

Visit **marsvenuscoaching.com/bookbonus** to access your bonuses now.

EVERYTHING WE NEED IS ALREADY WITHIN US

PETRA ZAVAŠNIK

Petra Zavašnik is a Slovenian Mars Venus life and relationship coach, certified alongside her husband in 2024. With a passion for holistic well-being and a background as a biology professor, she specializes in guiding individuals toward sustainable, healthy weight loss and a balanced approach to life transformation.

As a certified hypnotic master practitioner, master NLP practitioner, and life and business coach, Petra creates a safe and supportive environment where individuals can build confidence, resilience, and long-term success through personal growth.

Petra's expertise is deeply personal. Having lost 61 pounds of body weight in a healthy and sustainable way, she understands the physical, emotional, and psychological challenges of transformation. Her approach isn't just about achieving goals but about redefining self-worth, building a healthier lifestyle, and fostering a positive relationship with one's body and mind.

With warmth and a gentle presence, Petra creates a space where individuals can slow down, reconnect with themselves, and release the weight of pressure, doubt, or past expectations. In this space, transformation doesn't come from force, but from awareness and clarity. She invites her clients to return to who they truly are—beyond roles, stories, or limitations.

Whether someone is navigating change in relationships, business, or personal growth, Petra offers both structure and space, allowing each person to explore what truly matters to them. Through grounded support and meaningful reflection, clients gain the confidence to move forward with greater self-trust, resilience, and alignment.

THE INVISIBLE TRANSFORMATION

As a coach, I've learned that every client is different—and I genuinely enjoy those differences. I'm deeply grateful and humbled each time someone invites me into their world.

My coaching is rooted in acceptance, nonjudgment, and a grounded, supportive presence. In that space, clients naturally feel safe to open up, in their own way, in their own time. I don't take that trust for granted—it's an honor to walk beside someone on their journey.

Coaching isn't about giving answers—it's about asking the right questions at the right time. It's about creating a space where insight can arise naturally, where a person feels safe enough to pause, reflect, and access their own inner wisdom. The right question, offered with presence and intention, opens the space for clarity.

In my coaching, I focus on helping clients lose weight healthily and sustainably. Weight loss isn't a one-time project—it's a lifelong relationship with ourselves. After all, we eat throughout our entire lives, and our bodies are the vehicles that carry us throughout our journey. It only makes sense that we learn how to take care of them in a way that supports us in all areas of life.

If you ask most people about how to lose weight, they can usually name at least one diet or strategy. The knowledge is out there. And yet, only a small percentage of people manage to lose weight in a way that's healthy and sustainable. That's because the challenge isn't just physical; it's emotional, mental, and deeply personal. And that's exactly why it's such a powerful opportunity—a chance to build inner strength, experience more freedom, and reconnect with our true selves.

It all begins with a decision, a commitment to care for your body. While many people make the New Year's resolution to lose weight and improve their health (often for the fifth year in a row!), they're often not prepared for the reality that follows. Our brains aren't wired to dive into change easily, especially when results don't come immediately. And when it comes to losing weight in a healthy way, quick results just aren't realistic.

After the decision, the next step requires courage—and courage rarely feels comfortable. That's where I come in.

As a coach, I help people recognize and release emotional blocks, embrace self-acceptance, and understand that there's no "right" or "wrong" way to approach a challenge. The path is exactly what it needs to be. And that's OK.

Among the many powerful client journeys I've had the honor to witness, one stands out: a man who came to me at age 50, quietly carrying the belief that weight loss simply wasn't possible for him. He had never lost weight in his life. Over the years, especially after certain life challenges and emotional traumas, his weight steadily increased. He described the process using the well-known metaphor of the frog in hot water: if the temperature rises slowly, the frog doesn't notice until it's too late. That's how weight gain felt for him—gradual, unnoticed, and eventually overwhelming.

By the time he reached out for coaching, he had already tried many diets. Each one ended in disappointment. As he told me later, he had stopped believing that change was possible, yet some part of him must have still carried a quiet hope … because he showed up.

Throughout our work together, we didn't just focus on food or habits. We explored limiting beliefs, emotional blocks, and unconscious patterns that had kept him stuck. Session by session, he began to reconnect with his strength, rebuild self-confidence, and discover that he could face his emotions, rather than avoid them.

The result? He started to take care of himself from a place of awareness and inner stability. He no longer felt dependent on external circumstances. He began responding differently to familiar situations, and people around him noticed. And yes, for the first time in his life, he lost weight—39 pounds and counting. But as he often says himself, the physical transformation is just the visible part. The real change happened within.

WEIGHT LOSS—WHAT SOME PEOPLE GET WRONG

Many people have misconceptions about weight loss. One day, while sitting in the waiting room for my youngest daughter's eye exam, I struck up a conversation with a woman sitting nearby. We chatted for a bit, and she shared her thoughts on weight: "Being thin isn't an issue, you just need to keep an eye on how much you eat now and then. We're all in the same boat—anyone can manage it by not overeating all the time."

I see where she's coming from, and I agree to some extent, but her statement was a bit of a generalization. Food definitely plays a big role in our daily calorie intake—but it's not quite that straightforward.

Understanding the many factors that influence a person's body weight can be truly enlightening. While diet and exercise are important, they're only part of the picture. Genetics, metabolism, sleep quality, stress levels, and overall lifestyle choices also play a major role. By exploring these influences, we gain a deeper understanding of our bodies and what they truly need to maintain balance—not just in weight, but in overall well-being.

For example, genetics can influence how easily someone gains or loses weight, how their body stores fat, and how their appetite is regulated.

Metabolism (how efficiently the body converts food into energy) varies from person to person and plays a big role in how the body responds to food and movement.

Then there's sleep, which affects key hormones related to hunger and fullness. When we're sleep-deprived, levels of ghrelin (which increases appetite) go up, while leptin (which signals fullness) drops. This hormonal shift can make it harder to make nourishing choices, even with the best intentions.

Stress also has a powerful impact. High levels of the stress hormone cortisol can lead to stronger cravings, emotional eating, and fat storage—especially around the belly area.

And finally, our lifestyle (how we eat, move, rest, and manage our emotions) shapes how all these pieces come together. It's not about perfection, but about creating a rhythm that supports us long term.

When we start to look at weight through a wider lens, it

becomes less about strict control and more about deeper understanding, self-kindness, and gentle change.

REWRITE YOUR STORY ON YOUR TERMS

At first glance, our physical appearance might seem less important than other areas of life, like personal growth or relationships. And while it's true that we're so much more than our bodies, the relationships we have with our bodies still matter deeply.

When someone doesn't fully accept their body, that inner conflict can quietly affect every part of their life—their confidence, relationships, even their professional path. True self-acceptance includes accepting the body we live in.

> **Feeling at home in ourselves, physically and emotionally, lays the foundation for connection, presence, and aligned action.**

Many people aren't living their full potential—not because they aren't capable, but because they don't believe they are. When someone has tried to lose weight for years and has failed, they may begin to believe it's simply not possible for them. And if that belief becomes embedded in one area of life, it often spreads silently into others, limiting what they believe they can achieve, deserve, or become.

Often, we live from our past. From what we were told, what

we learned to believe, and what we made those experiences mean about us. We carry these old beliefs as if they're absolute truths, without realizing that someone else, in the very same situation, might have felt and experienced it completely differently. Change can feel difficult, even unreachable. And so, we tell ourselves, *This is just who I am*. But that's not the truth—it's just a story. We all carry stories—about who we are, what we're capable of, and what's possible for us. Some of those stories empower us. Others quietly limit us. And like all stories, they can be rewritten.

As a coach, I help clients recognize the stories that no longer serve them and explore what's possible when they choose to write new narratives grounded in clarity, self-trust, and inner freedom. We're more moldable than we think. When we learn to leave past limitations, beliefs, and heavy experiences where they belong—in the past—we begin to reclaim the present. This is where real transformation happens. Through awareness, gentle practice, and supportive guidance, we can start to live from who we truly are, rather than from who we were taught to be.

Ultimately, success looks different for everyone, because we're not all here to walk the same path. One of the most freeing things we can do is stop measuring ourselves against someone else's journey. That's why inner success matters most. When we're rooted in peace, aligned with who we truly are, and clear about what's meaningful to us, external success naturally becomes more genuine, more sustainable—and truly ours.

BUT WHAT ABOUT GENDER INTELLIGENCE?

You might be thinking, *Physical and psychological transformations are great ... but where does gender intelligence fit in all this?* To be honest, becoming a Mars Venus coach wasn't something I initially planned or felt particularly drawn to. I enrolled in the program because my husband invited me. I had no idea what to expect—but I was pleasantly surprised.

What impacted me most was realizing just *how different* men and women truly are in their everyday lives. While I had some awareness of these differences, the Mars Venus philosophy brought a deeper understanding that completely shifted my perspective. I learned that with willingness and the right tools, relationships of any kind can be transformed. Gender intelligence applies everywhere: in the workplace, in society, in everyday communication. Any woman can learn how to speak in a way that builds connection with a man, and the same goes for men who want to connect more deeply with women.

In our household, there's always something that needs to be done—chores that my husband, truth be told, often does better than I do.

Before Mars Venus Coaching, I used to ask him for help at moments when he wasn't prepared—perhaps he was already focused on something else or doing something important. Naturally, he wasn't thrilled by my request, and I would feel disappointed at his response. My interpretation back then? *He doesn't want to do things that matter to me.* At the same time, I would often wait and wait—secretly hoping for the "right" moment—until the need felt urgent. But because I was rarely satisfied with his response, the tension kept building.

Then I learned how to ask in the Martian way.

To ask a man for help in a way that works well, it's helpful to keep the request simple, respectful, and clear. One way is to start by asking, "Would you do me a favor?" and wait for his response. Then, make the request with a calm and relaxed tone—for example, "Would you please change the light bulb later today?" Adding a gentle time frame like "later today" gives him space to choose when to do it, which helps the request feel less like pressure and more like an invitation. It's helpful to speak in a warm and appreciative way that invites cooperation. Saying something like, "It would mean a lot to me" shows that his help truly matters and makes him feel appreciated. Or, "It would make me really happy" so he can feel successful and valued for doing something that brings her joy. This approach leads to more openness, willingness, and connection on both sides.

What a relief! Once I learned the Mars Venus methods, suddenly there was little to no tension in our relationship. And if there was any, I no longer took it personally. My husband still does things in his own time—but they get done. It turns out … he actually loves doing things for me. And I genuinely enjoy thanking him in the way *he* prefers.

Learning gender intelligence not only improved communication between me and my husband, but also between me and my clients. Learning to speak the "language" of the other gender is an act of love and respect, not strategy. It opens the door to deeper understanding, softens miscommunication, and builds trust. When we learn how the other person gives and receives connection, we're better able to meet their needs—not from obligation, but from genuine care. It's not about changing who we are, but about creating space for everyone to feel seen, heard, and valued.

TRANSFORMATION REQUIRES EFFORT

Some people ask me if there are clients I can't work with. My answer is simple: yes—the ones who don't want to be worked with. But when someone chooses to invest their time, energy, and resources into coaching with me, it tells me there's already a wish for change, even if it's quiet at first. And that's enough to begin.

One of the most valuable things I've learned is how to adapt my communication style—how to really *connect* with people. I know how to build rapport, how to approach someone in a way that makes them feel safe, seen, and open. Whether someone's seeking support in their personal life or professional world, I meet them where they are so they can receive what they truly need from the coaching process. In that space, they receive my full attention and presence, along with the right questions—ones that gently lead them inward. From there, new perspectives begin to unfold.

And when perspective shifts, the path toward the change

they desire becomes clear and reachable. I feel deeply honored to be invited into someone's reality, and to walk with them toward the life they long for.

My coaching is grounded in deep listening—not just to words, but to what's beneath them. I listen for emotion, for insight, for the lens through which someone sees their life. The way you listen can be more loving than the way you speak, especially when you're not quietly preparing your reply, but simply being present, listening without needing to defend, fix, or respond. Just holding space for the other person to be heard. And when someone comes to me with a goal that seems external, like a number or a result, I look deeper. What's underneath that? What feeling is truly driving the desire for change?

Life often speaks in whispers at first—through subtle emotions, quiet tension, or an inner knowing that something needs attention. If we're present enough to notice, those small signals can guide us before the whispers need to get louder. It's not about getting everything right or perfect. Life doesn't demand perfection—it simply asks us to stay present, stay connected, and be willing to listen to what our emotions are trying to tell us about ourselves.

As a coach, I guide people in learning how to communicate with themselves in a stronger, clearer way. Because the way we speak to ourselves shapes how we live. Weak inner dialogue creates a weak life, whereas strong, honest communication creates strength.

Everyone can ask themselves: *Is my life the way I want it to be?* **And if the answer is no, that's not failure—it's an invitation. An opportunity for more ease, more emotional freedom, and a state of being that supports creating in every area of life.**

When I coach clients, we explore truly lasting motivation. Fear-based or pressure-based motivation fades quickly. Therefore, I guide people in developing the ability to take the steps that truly matter for long-term change. Trust in their abilities—and in the possibility of success—doesn't come first. It's built along the way. And when it does come, something beautiful happens: they become unstoppable. They know they can do it. They're connected to an inner motivation that doesn't depend on external circumstances.

My work is to help someone connect with their inner fire—the deep desire that can carry them toward real and lasting transformation. I hold up the bigger picture for them: What else might be possible? What lies beyond what they currently believe? Together, we step into inner success—freedom, peace, alignment, clarity, and purpose. Along the way, we celebrate their victories, both big and small. And in that process, they begin to see their own strength, truth, and potential more clearly than ever before. It's a journey of remembering who they truly are and stepping into their potential. It all starts with acceptance.

How you relate to yourself shapes how others learn to relate to you. No one can truly fill the space inside you that you haven't first learned to hold with love. Love isn't something to chase or earn—it's something to remember. It's not a destination, but a way of being. The love you're searching for outside of you is already within you. When you begin to see yourself through the eyes of love, you realize that you don't need to become anything more. You are love. You always were.

> "Men and women often speak different emotional languages. What brings relief and connection to one can trigger misunderstanding in the other. When we learn to decode these differences, conflict gives way to compassion."
>
> **DR. JOHN GRAY**

THE WORLD IS BUILT ON RELATIONSHIPS

SAMUEL SINGER

Rabbi Samuel Singer is a dedicated relationship counselor specializing in couples therapy. His journey began with navigating a difficult childhood, an experience that fueled his passion for growth, resilience, and helping others overcome their own challenges. At just 19 years old, he earned his first rabbinical degree, marking the beginning of over a decade of intensive study that deepened his understanding of human relationships, personal development, and spiritual wisdom.

Rabbi Singer's approach to counseling is holistic, emphasizing personal responsibility rather than blame. He believes that true transformation comes from knowledge and awareness—keys that unlock personal and relational fulfillment. Rabbi Singer helps couples identify and overcome patterns that hold them back, guiding them toward deeper connection, mutual respect, and lasting love. His work integrates psychological principles with theological and philosophical insights, offering a balanced and meaningful perspective on relationships.

Beyond his counseling practice, Rabbi Singer has a strong passion for health and nutrition. Having studied these fields extensively, he understands the profound link between physical well-being and emotional resilience, and he encourages a lifestyle that supports both mental and relational health.

In addition to his counseling work, he is a prolific writer, regularly exploring themes of theology, philosophy, psychology, and self-improvement. Through his articles, he shares insights on relationships, personal growth, and deeper life questions.

Today, Rabbi Singer not only helps others build fulfilling relationships but also cherishes his own. He is grateful for the incredible bond he shares with his wife and four children, living out the very principles he teaches—love, awareness, and personal growth.

THE IMPORTANCE OF LOVE AND CONNECTION

I've always been fascinated by people—why we do what we do. But relationships, in particular, are my favorite area of study because they shape so much of our lives. Relationship coaching and maintaining emotional health are practices I engage in daily, whether at work, at home with my wife, with my children, with friends, or in business. Essentially, the practice of strengthening relationships is a constant in my life, except when I'm asleep.

Working with people, I've seen how a loving relationship affects every aspect of a person's well-being. For example, if someone is rude, it often reflects something about their relationship. If they're depressed, that too can often be traced back to their relationship. Most of the time, when people have a strong, loving connection with their spouse, they become kind, understanding, and grounded. From there, it can grow into other areas of life, including work and even global influence. Rarely do you see a kind husband being a nasty employer or politician; it's like you have to start cleaning your own house before you clean others'. Often, we see people talking about world peace or animal rights, but these people often come across as rude or narcissistic.

> We need to start our agendas of love and peace from the inside out, not the outside in.

In general, healthy relationships create people whom others enjoy being around. On the other hand, people who stay isolated for too long often become bitter, self-centered, and rigid in their thinking.

When helping clients build stronger, more fulfilling relationships, gender intelligence is invaluable—because if we don't recognize that people are different, we cannot truly understand or respect them. Expecting others to be just like us is a form of narcissism. Do you only like others when they're like you? When we marry someone, we should expect them to be different from us. However, instead of appreciating these differences, people often complain about them and look for strategies, such as conflict resolution and communication techniques, to "even the playing field." While these strategies have their place, the real key to a successful relationship is understanding that our spouses are supposed to be different. Marriage is about coming together as two distinct individuals with unique perspectives, tastes, and preferences. This, in turn, helps us grow as individuals. As the saying goes, "Marriage is not a hospital," but in many ways, it can still be therapy, or maybe homeopathy. A committed relationship helps us become the best version of ourselves, *if* we can make it work.

In today's world, where people struggle to accept differing opinions, it's no coincidence that marriages have suffered. And as marriages suffer, society becomes more polarized. A loving marriage fosters emotional health and openness to new ideas, creating the safest and healthiest space for the genesis of new life—the next generation. So not only does a committed relationship develop our best selves, but it's also the best space to create new life. Studies have consistently shown that children raised in two-parent homes, where the father loves the mother and the mother trusts the father, tend to be the healthiest both mentally and emotionally. Every child is made of three parts: one part from the mother, one part from the father, and the third part is their godliness or spirituality. These three parts are our male qualities, our female qualities, and our unique self. When any one of these three elements is distorted, it creates distortion in the person as a whole. Even in cases of divorce, children tend to grow up more mentally stable when both parents remain actively involved in their upbringing.

Epidemiological studies have examined the effects of two-parent homes on children using both cross-sectional and longitudinal study designs. Research suggests that children raised by both parents experience lower rates of depression and anxiety. For example, a study published by the University of Cambridge highlights the influence of parenting practices on the mental health of both parents and children over time.[12] Additionally, studies on shared parenting emphasize its positive effects on children following divorce.[13]

The power of a two-parent home is well-documented, and gender intelligence is a valuable tool for building and maintaining strong, enduring relationships. It allows us to generalize and categorize differences in a way that makes sense to everyone. While we can never fully capture every individual's uniqueness, it is essential to recognize that differences are natural and necessary. Embracing these differences strengthens relationships and builds a healthier, more accepting society.

The wisdom of gender intelligence is based on common sense and human success—it's not necessarily a hard science. In fact, in today's world, a PhD can sometimes be a disadvantage when it comes to understanding relationships. What makes you successful in the lab doesn't necessarily make you successful at home. Similarly, the tactics that work in business to achieve success don't always translate to success in love. Formal education doesn't necessarily teach common sense, and at the end of the day, successful relationships depend on exactly that—*common sense*. Although there's plenty of scientific evidence to back the Mars Venus methods, it's not the entire picture. Mars Venus's unique philosophy is also based on the experiences of thousands and thousands of people—*real* people in *real* relationships.

Having a career that centers on relationships is great because you can practice them with friends and everyone around you. Can you be an investigator at home? No! Try being an investigator at home—it's a recipe for disaster. It's a good job, but not a successful approach to love. How about a programmer? Nope, that's not good at home either. To build healthy relationships, you must take the right approach, and Mars Venus provides practical, real-world insights that make love and connection accessible to everyone.

USING SCIENTIFIC INSIGHTS TO ENLIGHTEN CLIENTS

In my practice, I take a holistic, multidisciplinary approach to coaching, integrating Mars Venus techniques with trauma-informed methods, CBT (cognitive behavioral therapy), EFT (emotionally focused therapy), and a strong emphasis on health. I don't simply treat symptoms or label issues; I work with individuals as whole human beings, focusing on their unique needs and offering tools that can truly transform their lives. My aim is not just to help people fix a problem but to empower them to become stronger, more self-aware versions of themselves, even if they might be younger or less experienced in navigating personal growth.

In my approach, I focus on explaining the science behind emotional responses and behaviors. By helping clients understand how the brain functions and how past experiences shape their reactions, we create a clear path toward healing. Just like a doctor explains the effects and purpose of medication, I explain how our work together impacts the brain and body, allowing clients to better understand the process and make progress in the intended direction.

Sarah and Eli had been attending therapy for several weeks, making steady progress. While Eli, a practical and intelligent computer technician, understood the concepts we were discussing, the emotional weight of Sarah's triggers still seemed to elude him. We had already delved into Sarah's past and learned she had a history of abandonment issues. In this particular session, we were discussing that each time Eli would go out with friends, Sarah would react as if it were a deep betrayal. Sarah was visibly upset. "It feels like you're choosing them over me," she said, her voice shaking.

Eli, frustrated, responded, "I love you, Sarah. But I need time with my friends. Can't you just understand that?"

I could tell Eli wasn't fully grasping how deep Sarah's reactions went. "Eli," I began, "I know this seems simple to you, but Sarah's body is responding to something much deeper. It's not just about you going out; it's about old wounds being triggered."

Eli looked at me, confused. "But she should just get over it, right?"

Explaining rationally clearly wasn't working, so I pulled up an image of a man with a broken leg. "When you see this image, would you tell this person to just get up and walk, as if nothing's wrong?"

"No," Eli said, looking puzzled. "He's injured."

"Exactly," I said, switching to a brain scan image of a person impacted by childhood trauma. "Now, look at this. This is what happens when a child experiences trauma. The brain doesn't just bounce back like a normal brain—it's impacted, just like a physical injury."

Eli's eyes widened as he processed the image. "Oh ... I get it now. It's like she's injured in a way I can't see."

"Right," I said. "Sarah's reactions are not overreactions. Her brain has been wired to respond this way. It's not something she can control without help."

Using brain scans to show Eli how trauma can alter brain function, similar to how a physical injury affects movement, I helped him understand that Sarah's emotional reactions were rooted in past experiences, not just the present situation. With this understanding, we developed strategies to help Sarah process these triggers and support her in feeling safe.

ALL PROGRESS STARTS WITH ACCEPTING RESPONSIBILITY

As a coach, one of my most significant challenges is guiding people to a place where they can truly accept help. It's not uncommon for individuals to be defensive, and this often stems from a deeper reluctance to open up, especially when the guidance is coming from someone younger than them. The truth is, accepting help requires strength—strength to be vulnerable, to let go of control, and to trust that someone else can offer valuable insight.

A core philosophy of Mars Venus is taking responsibility. We know that it takes two to fight. The flip side of that is that it takes only one to keep the peace and be loving. In any relationship, rarely is there a time when one partner can't do something to rectify the situation. We call them relationships for a reason—it's about how we *relate* to others. When people struggle in relationships, they often blame their partner, or their partner's friends or family—anyone but themselves. They rarely see it as their own responsibility. The problem is that many people equate responsibility with blame, which makes them defensive. When someone is defensive, it's difficult to reach them, educate them, or help them become aware of what they can change.

But responsibility doesn't mean blame—it means you have the power to change things. If you break down the word, it becomes "response-ability," meaning the ability to respond. It's not about accepting fault; it's about recognizing that even if something isn't your fault, you still have the ability to do something about it. If you don't embrace that power, you become defensive, shut down, or run from the problem, which only makes it worse. The key is to ask yourself: *How did I contribute to this issue? How can I change my response to improve the situation?*

In *Men Are from Mars, Women Are from Venus*, the focus isn't on fixing your partner—it's on understanding them. Understanding someone allows you to shape your life around that awareness rather than trying to change them. It doesn't teach you how to fix them; rather, it shifts the *response-ability* onto you.

> **When you truly understand another person, you gain the ability to respond in a way that nurtures the relationship, rather than expecting them to change to meet your needs.**

Another crucial aspect of *response-ability* is recognizing that your happiness is your own responsibility. You need to build a fulfilling life for yourself first, and then bring your spouse into it. Relying on your partner to make you happy is no different from relying on money for happiness—true fulfillment doesn't come from external sources. If you aren't happy and content within yourself, no relationship can fill that void.

LOVE IS THE HEART OF LIFE

Ultimately, I wish everyone understood the power of love and relationships, especially a monogamous relationship. To have a loving relationship is like the center of the Earth—it's the foundation from which we begin to change people's lives and, eventually, the world for the better. Love must first exist in our own lives before we can have a broader positive impact.

Love directly affects our ability to handle stress; it's a biological fact. For instance, married men tend to be less competitive—getting married literally changes the brain.[14] We all know that the initial rush of falling in love is like taking a drug, putting us in an altered state. In the past, it was accepted that, in long-term relationships, the passion would eventually die. Sigmund Freud even went so far as to suggest that sustained passion in long-term relationships isn't typical and may indicate pathology (a psychological fixation rather than a healthy attachment).[15] However, with good relationship practices, the effects of love can be long-lasting, and we can keep the passion alive.

Research on long-term romantic love has found sustained

activation in brain regions linked to reward and motivation. A study published in the *Journal of Neurophysiology* showed that individuals in long-term loving relationships exhibit significant activity in the ventral tegmental area, a dopamine-rich region associated with pleasure and reward. This neural activity mirrors that seen in early-stage romantic love, suggesting that deep love can continue to shape the brain over time.[16] The findings contradict the common belief that romantic passion inevitably declines over time.

Additionally, women in the workplace experience higher stress levels than men.[17] However, the anticipation of love and support from a spouse significantly lowers that stress.[18] Often, love really is the answer.

Love isn't just an emotional experience—it's a biological and psychological force that shapes our well-being, resilience, and ability to create meaningful change in the world. Love is associated with the heart, and much like the heart, it keeps us alive.

> "Relationships don't just survive on love—they thrive with ongoing attention, understanding, and appreciation."
>
> **DR. JOHN GRAY**

THE HEART OF TEAMWORK

Love, Communication, and Gender Intelligence

MONIQUE SARUP

As a relationship and mindset coach, Monique's mission is to help women create strong, thriving partnerships by first building their own confidence and voice within the relationship. She guides women to communicate more openly, set healthy boundaries, and nurture teamwork in their homes so love feels like a source of strength rather than stress.

Having begun her self-development journey at the age of nine, Monique now draws on those lifelong skills in her adult life as a wife, mother, and coach. She understands the importance of women recognizing their emotions, strengthening communication, and living with clarity of purpose—not just for themselves, but also for their families.

Monique has "walked the talk," applying the same mindset techniques she teaches to nurture her marriage, raise her children, and create a balanced, supportive home. She understands the unique pressures women face today: carrying the weight of family responsibilities, building a career, and often putting their own needs last, all while striving to maintain meaningful connection with their partners. Through personalized coaching and proven relationship strategies, she helps women reclaim their sense of worth, rediscover intimacy, and cultivate balance across both work and home life. Monique also emphasizes the importance of self-love and self-care, showing women how to prioritize themselves so they don't burn out, and instead model what healthy love, balance, and resilience look like for their children.

At the heart of her work is the belief that when a woman learns to strengthen herself and her relationships, she doesn't just change her own life; she changes the legacy of love and connection she passes on to her family.

FALLING IN LOVE VS. STAYING IN LOVE

Marriage has been one of my greatest teachers. As much as my personal development journey began in childhood, it's within the walls of my marriage and the rhythm of family life that I've discovered the deepest lessons about love, teamwork, and communication.

As a married mother of three, every day I'm reminded that relationships aren't about perfection. They're about presence, understanding, and choosing to work together, even when it isn't easy. Love isn't just the spark that begins a relationship; it's the daily actions, the conversations, and the choices that keep it alive.

When I first met my husband, falling in love felt effortless. There were butterflies, long conversations, laughter, and that magnetic pull that makes you believe you've found your person. But as life unfolded—marriage, children, careers, and the daily responsibilities of running a household—that effortless spark needed more intentional care. But I soon learned that *staying in love* isn't about butterflies—it's about building.

In the beginning, I thought love would simply carry us. I imagined a steady path upward: marriage, family, happiness. The reality was much more complex. Love gave us the foundation, but it was communication, compromise, and conscious effort that built the structure of our marriage, all fueled by our understanding of gender intelligence.

The first time my husband and I disagreed about something major, I felt almost betrayed. *Shouldn't we be on the same page about everything?* But marriage quickly taught me that disagreement is normal. It's how you *handle* it that determines the strength of the relationship.

COMMUNICATION: MORE THAN WORDS

In our early days, I believed I was a good communicator. After all, I grew up in a coaching household. I had the tools, the awareness, and the language. But with typical work and family demands, we were tested.

I discovered that communication isn't about how clearly you can explain your own perspective; it's about how deeply you can listen to your partner's.

> **Listening isn't just nodding; it's leaning in with empathy. It's not preparing your next rebuttal, but really hearing what your partner is saying—and sometimes what they're *not* saying.**

One of the most transformative shifts came when I stopped saying, "You always" or "You never" and started saying, "I feel." That one adjustment turned defensiveness into openness. Instead of making accusations, we began having conversations.

This ties directly into Dr. John Gray's Mars Venus teachings. Men and women communicate differently based on not just social conditioning but also biology. Women's stress levels reduce when they feel heard and validated, while men's stress lowers when they feel effective and capable. When I learned to say, "I just need you to listen right now, not fix it," it freed my husband to simply be present. And when he began to share his challenges, I practiced listening without layering emotional judgment. This shift transformed countless conversations.

THE POWER OF TEAMWORK

Raising three children has shown me the importance of teamwork on a whole new level.

There are late nights with sick children, early mornings, endless activities, and the juggle of careers and household responsibilities. No matter how organized we try to be, there are always unexpected moments that throw the schedule off-balance.

> **Teamwork in marriage doesn't always mean splitting everything down the middle. Instead, it's about embracing the natural strengths each partner brings to the relationship.**

As women, we're often the nurturers—the ones who bring warmth, emotional connection, and the ability to sense when our families need comfort or encouragement. Men, on the other hand, often step naturally into the role of leaders and protectors, offering strength, direction, and stability when challenges arise.

When the baby wouldn't stop crying, my husband's calm, steady presence brought a sense of security into our home. This is a classic example of how men, in their masculine energy, often respond to stress by becoming more solution-focused and steady. His quiet strength communicated safety to me and to the children.

When our toddlers were learning to share toys or struggling with big feelings they couldn't yet put into words, it was my nurturing heart and coaching skills that helped navigate those situations. Women, in their feminine energy, often excel at emotional connection. By listening, validating, and gently guiding our children through those moments, I was teaching not only patience and kindness but also the language of empathy.

From a Mars Venus perspective, both roles are essential. Children don't just need discipline or calm problem-solving; they also need emotional coaching and nurturing. When men and women honor their different strengths—for example, a man's steady presence and a woman's emotional guidance—we create a complete environment where children feel both safe and understood.

The lesson for parents is: instead of trying to do it all the same way, recognise and value the natural differences between genders. While men and women may respond differently, together they provide the balance kids need to thrive. In any one moment, the balance is rarely perfect, but in the long run, honoring our differences creates harmony—a partnership where both roles are equally valued and essential. It's about understanding each other's needs, even when they're not openly expressed.

After our third child was born, I hit a wall of exhaustion. Sleepless nights, two toddlers still needing attention, everyone wanting their mum, and the demands of being in business leaving me drained. My husband, who also runs a business and works long days, quietly began taking over Sunday morning breakfast and activities so I could sleep in and start my day differently from every other day of the week. He didn't make a big deal about it; he just noticed I was struggling and stepped in. That small act of teamwork didn't just help me—it reminded me I wasn't alone.

MODELING LOVE FOR OUR CHILDREN

Children learn far more from what they see than from what they're told. I can talk to my kids about respect, kindness, and love, but the most powerful lessons come from what they witness in their daily lives.

When they see my husband and I hug in the kitchen, apologize after an argument, or laugh together at the dinner table, they're learning what healthy love looks like. When they hear us talk through challenges calmly, they learn that disagreement doesn't equal disrespect. And when they watch us forgive, they learn that mistakes are simply part of every relationship.

I'll never forget the day our eldest came to me after witnessing an argument and said, "Mum, I saw you and Dad yelling, but then you hugged after. Does that mean you're OK now?" In that moment, I realized just how closely children absorb the way we relate. Now, whenever my husband and I disagree, we let them see us apologize and reconnect. It's not about avoiding conflict—it's about modeling resolution.

But modeling love isn't just about how we treat each other. It's also about how we treat ourselves. When my children see me take time for a walk, set healthy boundaries, or speak kindly to myself instead of being overly critical, they're learning that self-love matters too. Self-love isn't selfish; it's the foundation that allows us to love others well. A child who grows up seeing their parents honor their own needs and well-being will grow into an adult who respects themselves and their relationships. Having my own hobbies, social life, and time to fill my cup isn't only beneficial for me; it also shows my children it's healthy, and they're allowed, to nurture their own passions and well-being too.

From a Mars Venus perspective, love is shown and received in different ways. Women often feel loved through affection, connection, and being listened to, while men often feel loved through respect, appreciation, and trust. By modeling both, offering affection and connection, while also showing respect and appreciation, we're giving our children a living example of balanced love. And by pairing this with self-love, caring for ourselves, respecting our limits, and practicing forgiveness inwardly, we show them that love isn't just something you give away; it's something you also give to yourself.

Life in our home isn't perfect. Sometimes it's chaos; sometimes we raise our voices, and sometimes we get it wrong. But the foundation we come back to is the idea that children don't need perfect parents; they need authentic parents. By showing them that love includes self-care, hard conversations, compromises, and forgiveness, we're equipping them with tools for their own future relationships and, most importantly, the belief that they too are worthy of love.

DIFFERENT PATHS TO CALM

One of the most eye-opening insights from the Mars Venus teachings is how men and women process stress differently.

When my husband is stressed, he often retreats into quiet. He'll spend time listening to music, cooking outside in the barbeque, watching a show, or simply being silent. In the early days, I took this personally. I thought his silence meant disinterest, or worse, disconnection. But I've since learned that this is how men rebuild testosterone, their primary stress-reducing hormone. Silence and problem-solving *restore* him.

For me as a woman, stress relief comes through talking, connection, and being heard. When I'm upset, I want to share every detail, every feeling, and I want empathy in return. This releases oxytocin and lowers cortisol.

Once we understood this difference, we stopped taking each other's coping mechanisms personally. I learned to give him space without feeling abandoned. He learned to listen without feeling pressured to solve. This small shift prevented countless misunderstandings and deepened our trust.

STRATEGIES THAT STRENGTHEN OUR MARRIAGE

Through our journey, I've gathered a tool kit of strategies that help us maintain connection:

- **Scheduled time together:** Between kids and careers, we schedule time for *just us*. It's not unromantic—it's intentional.
- **The power of appreciation:** A simple "thank you for doing the dishes" carries more weight than we realize.
- **Repairing quickly:** Disagreements happen, but we don't let them linger. A hug, an apology, or a shared laugh helps us reset.
- **Dividing roles, but not rigidly:** We play to our strengths, but we're flexible when life demands it.
- **Prioritizing self-care:** We've learned that looking after ourselves individually is just as important as looking after our relationship. When I fill my own cup—whether it's through exercise, journaling, or quiet time—I show up more patient and present. When my husband takes space to recharge, he comes back stronger and more engaged. By valuing self-care, we remind each other that love includes respecting our own needs too.
- **Speaking the other's language:** My husband thrives

on respect as the leader of our family, while I thrive on empathy as the nurturer. By honoring these roles, we give each other what we need and model balance for our children.

These aren't complicated practices, but they're powerful when done consistently.

GROWTH THROUGH SEASONS

Every marriage has seasons. Some are full of sunshine and ease; others feel like long winters. There are seasons of romance, seasons of survival, and seasons of renewal.

What keeps us going is the decision to grow together. As individuals, we've both changed. The young adults who fell in love years ago aren't the same people parenting three kids today. But by sharing our growth, rather than growing apart, we've created a stronger bond.

Marriage has taught me that love isn't about avoiding hardship, but about facing it side by side. It's not about always agreeing, but about respecting differences. And it's not about grand gestures, but about the everyday choices to listen, support, and choose each other again and again.

You might be thinking, *Why is the focus on a happy marriage? Isn't there more in life than just your partner?* I see a happy marriage, along with self-love, as foundational because a romantic relationship doesn't just impact the two people in it; it spills into every other area of life. When our relationship is strong, we parent with more patience, show up to work with more focus, and handle life's challenges with more resilience. When we're connected at home, we have the energy to pursue our dreams, the courage to take risks, and the support to bounce back when things go wrong. Our children benefit from seeing what genuine love looks like; our businesses thrive because we're not weighed down by unresolved conflict, and even our health improves because stress is lowered and joy is higher.

From a Mars Venus perspective, happiness comes when both partners feel loved in the way they most need it. Men thrive when they feel respected and appreciated; women thrive when they feel heard and emotionally connected. When these needs are met, both partners bring their best selves not only to the marriage, but to every other role they play in life.

When love is built on teamwork, communication, and the freedom to grow, it doesn't just enrich our marriage; it becomes the foundation for a fulfilling family life, thriving careers, better health, and a legacy of love and resilience that carries forward for generations. This foundation, strengthened with *personal love*, creates wholeness. Because while a strong marriage is vital, it can only flourish when each partner also honors themselves. Self-love is the fuel that allows us to keep giving without burning out. When I take care of my mind, body, and spirit, I can show up with patience and presence. When my husband invests in his own well-being and sense of purpose, he shows up with energy and strength.

Without self-love, we risk leaning too heavily on each other to fill the gaps. But with it, we bring two whole, grounded individuals into the marriage, making the connection richer, deeper, and more resilient. Our children don't just see parents who love each other; they see parents who love themselves enough to set healthy boundaries, prioritize well-being, and keep growing. It's this balance that truly sustains love through every season of life.

> "The success of a relationship is solely dependent on two factors: a man's ability to listen lovingly and respectfully to a woman's feelings, and a woman's ability to share her feelings in a loving and respectful way."
>
> **DR. JOHN GRAY**

UNLOCK EXCLUSIVE BONUS CONTENT!

Dr. John Gray and his certified coaches have created powerful resources to enhance your understanding of gender intelligence and the wider Mars Venus philosophy.

Inside your free bonus pack, you'll get:
- Audio downloads
- Printable worksheets
- Practical tools and resources—and more!

Visit **marsvenuscoaching.com/bookbonus** to access your bonuses now.

LIFE AND LOVE ARE AN ADVENTURE

MALCOLM BRETT

Malcolm Brett is a certified Mars Venus life and relationship coach whose multifaceted background uniquely equips him to help clients build stronger, more fulfilling relationships. With extensive expertise in emotional well-being and physical health, Malcolm has dedicated his career to guiding individuals toward balanced and joyful lives. He is an intuitive healer and uses his very unique and powerful intuitive skills to gain clarity and insight into each individual client's situation, which is incredibly helpful for guiding them toward the goals and achievements they so richly deserve.

Since 1997, Malcolm has been an Edward Bach Australian bush flower therapist, employing kinesiology techniques to diagnose and treat emotional challenges. He integrates Dr. John Gray's emotional processing methods to help remove past traumas that create blocks, enabling clients to embrace the happiness they deserve. A lifelong practitioner of meditation, Malcolm has refined nearly five decades of experience into his own signature practice—Sky Heart Meditation—which he teaches to those seeking inner balance.

Earlier in his career, Malcolm balanced a dynamic role as an industrial fencing contractor by day with owner-builder responsibilities on weekends. These experiences honed his problem-solving skills and nurtured a passion for earth building—a pursuit that deepened his appreciation for homes that harmonize with nature. Today, he lives in his own handcrafted mud brick home on 2.2 hectares of land an hour from Brisbane, Australia.

An artist at heart, Malcolm finds creative expression through portraiture, working with oils, pastels, and pencils to capture the essence of his subjects.

Malcolm's journey into life and relationship coaching was born from personal growth and transformation. After years of navigating conflicts and misunderstandings in his own relationships, he sought answers and found them in Dr. John Gray's book *Beyond Mars and Venus*. His diverse expertise and holistic approach to coaching empower him to guide others toward meaningful relationships and more enriched, healthy, and joyful lives.

THE MOMENT THE PENNY DROPPED

After nearly a lifetime of rocky relationships, I realized something had to change, but I wasn't sure where to start. I became aware of the importance of gender intelligence after I developed an unexpected and powerful connection with a friend I had known for years. After more than 13 years of celibacy, it felt as if the carpet had been pulled out from under me. I had fallen in love, and just like that, everything I thought was settled came undone. The floodgates opened, and all the childhood traumas I had buried for years rose to the surface, demanding to be healed.

Thankfully, my friend had a background in psychology and had attended many relationship workshops. She generously shared her knowledge with me, offering insights that helped me navigate the intense emotions I was experiencing. Finally, when I watched a John Gray YouTube video, the penny dropped. His insights made sense on a deep level, and his teachings weren't just theories; they were practical, real-world strategies that explained so many of my past relationship struggles.

As I explored the Mars Venus philosophy, I saw the immense value in understanding gender intelligence, not just for nurturing a potential soulmate connection, but for strengthening all my relationships.

I realized that learning how men and women process emotions differently could be the key to deeper, more harmonious connections in every area of my life. Understanding the way men and women think differently is a game changer. Once you understand gender intelligence, you can see how men and women deal with stress differently. Instead of these differences being a source of confusion and conflict, they become a wonderful opportunity to create intimacy and bonding with your partner. Gender intelligence also helps you build better relationships with children, friends, acquaintances, and in the workplace. When you truly understand and appreciate our differences, communication becomes easier; misunderstandings decrease, and relationships naturally deepen. Gender intelligence fosters greater respect, empathy, and cooperation, making every interaction more harmonious and fulfilling, and enhancing our relationships.

Great relationships are electrifying, dynamic, and deeply rooted in both passion and friendship. The Mars-Venus dynamic reveals that the most powerful partnerships ignite with the fire of attraction but endure through unwavering connection. Mars energy infuses the relationship with bold decisiveness, fierce protection, and an unstoppable drive to solve problems, while Venus energy brings emotional richness, intuitive sensitivity, and open-hearted communication. When built on a solid foundation of friendship, this synergy transforms ordinary love into an extraordinary soulmate connection—one where respect, unwavering support, and a celebration of differences create an unbreakable bond. When both energies are fully embraced, love stops being just a feeling and becomes an unstoppable force, elevating the relationship to new heights of fulfillment and joy!

Love isn't just a feeling; it's an adventure, a dance, a journey of discovery. True love flourishes when the raw power of Mars and the radiant warmth of Venus intertwine. From a Mars perspective, love is bold, action-driven, and fearless, expressed through courageous acts, fierce devotion, and the willingness to take risks to protect and uplift a partner. From a Venus perspective, love is about deep, soul-nourishing empathy, heartfelt vulnerability, and the unconditional acceptance of a partner—flaws, quirks, and all. When both partners passionately embrace their natural energies—Mars fueling excitement and drive, Venus radiating tenderness and care—they forge a relationship that's not just resilient, but exhilarating. Love, in its most vibrant form, is about continually choosing each other, celebrating differences, and propelling each other toward a future filled with passion, happiness, connection, and limitless possibilities!

After discovering John Gray's work, I began taking his courses, and as I applied what I learned, I saw real improvements in my relationships. Encouraged by these changes, a friend suggested I consider becoming a Mars Venus coach. The idea clicked immediately. With a lifetime of experience across so many areas, I realized it was the perfect path for me. After a Zoom meeting with Richard Bernstein, the CEO and president of Mars Venus Coaching, I enrolled in the training program. Five months later, I was officially certified—and I haven't looked back. Becoming a Mars Venus coach has been one of the most rewarding decisions of my life. It not only transformed my own relationships but has also given me the tools to help others find deeper connection, understanding, and success in theirs.

THE HIDDEN HARM OF PARENTAL ALIENATION

When I coach clients on relationships, the focus isn't always romantic partnerships or professional relations. Sometimes we must work on their relationships with their children.

As a parental alienation expert and certified Mars Venus life and relationship coach, I help parents navigate the dynamics of this challenging situation. Parental alienation is an emotional abuse that can sever the bond between a parent and child. It happens when one parent manipulates a child to fear, reject, or avoid the other parent. This behavior, often rooted in unresolved trauma, can have long-lasting effects on both the child and the alienated parent.

It's very important to know that when you are interacting with a child in an alienation dynamic, you're not actually interacting with the child—you're interacting with a puppet or reflection of the alienating parent. The child then suffers from confusion, low self-esteem, and emotional turmoil, while the alienated parent faces profound loss and isolation.

My approach focuses on helping the alienated parent regain clarity, develop strategies, and take actionable steps to rebuild their relationship with their child. Together, we work to break the cycle of emotional abuse and restore the loving bond that once existed.

If you suspect you're dealing with parental alienation, I recommend watching "The Truth About Parental Alienation" by Teal Swan for more insight and support.[19]

CONQUERING FEAR OF CHANGE

As a coach, one of the biggest challenges I face is helping clients overcome their fear of change. Many people are deeply reluctant to take that first step toward a better life, often clinging to old patterns even when they no longer serve them. This resistance can feel like an obstacle, but it also presents an opportunity for real transformation.

My client Glen's journey with Mars Venus Coaching perfectly embodies the power of structured support, accountability, and a strong personal commitment. When he started coaching with me, he had three clear goals: clean his flat, finish his resin pour art projects, and improve his health through weight loss and more active social connections.

From day one, Glen was eager to engage with the process. He regularly filled out a "weekly focus sheet," a tool that helped him track his progress, clarify his priorities, and maintain focus. Cleaning his flat and completing his art projects were interconnected goals. His flat served as his creative studio, where he worked on intricate resin pour designs. By making his art a priority, he also worked toward creating a cleaner, more organized living space. This process emphasized that progress isn't always about speed; it's about consistent effort and maintaining high standards, even when things don't move as quickly as expected.

Glen's health journey was equally impactful. He tracked his weight daily, which helped him recognize patterns and identify the effects of his diet. By recording his meals, he naturally cut out junk food and focused on healthier choices. He also embraced a liver detox and started a regular exercise routine, which helped improve both his physical health and mindset.

Throughout our coaching sessions, we set realistic goals aligned with Glen's vision, and he found the practice of writing things down essential to staying motivated and disciplined. He also appreciated the support I provided—having a coach who genuinely cared about his progress made a huge difference.

Glen's journey is a reminder that, with consistent effort, small actions lead to big changes. His success reinforces why

I'm passionate about helping people achieve their goals and grow—but growth doesn't always come easily.

Fear of the unknown often paralyses clients, making them hesitant to commit to even small changes. They worry about the discomfort that change may bring and are skeptical of new approaches. Convincing them that Mars Venus coaching can not only improve their lives but also positively impact their relationships is key.

To help clients overcome their fear, I focus on building trust and rapport. I create a safe, supportive environment where they feel understood. By listening to their concerns and validating their feelings, I help them realize that their fears are normal and *can* be overcome.

Instead of pushing for drastic change, I introduce small, manageable steps. These incremental changes help shift a client's mindset, making the process less daunting. I also use visualization techniques to help them see a future where they feel happier, more confident, and successful. This vision motivates them to act.

THE ART OF ADAPTING TO CLIENT NEEDS

Through my holistic approach to coaching, I help bring clarity to every area and situation in my clients' lives. Using gender intelligence, I help men reconnect with their true masculine selves and women with their true feminine selves. This process balances hormones, reduces stress, and helps them better cope with the demands of modern life. But gender intelligence isn't the only coaching tool I employ.

By nature, I'm an intuitive healer. When I'm working with a client, I ask the right questions and feel the deep truth in their answers. From there, I generally have enough information to choose a healing path. For example, sometimes a client's goals are more practical, and there's less emotion involved, as was the case with Glen. In his case, we didn't need to delve too deeply into his emotions. Instead, we focused on motivation and practical steps to achieve his goals.

As a coach, it's important to adapt to each client's individual needs. While some people only require gentle guidance, others need additional support, whether that be through role-playing, kinesiology, or Australian bush flowers and Bach flower therapy, which is based on remedies Dr. Edward Bach developed in the 1930s. The remedies, taken orally, are derived from specific flowers, each flower producing a different effect—everything from raising self-awareness to helping develop self-esteem, assertiveness, self-discipline, and spontaneity and warmth in relationships. Working with the Bach flowers is like conspiring with nature to gain emotional well-being and security. Like blossoming flowers, we open up to a deeper understanding and appreciation of ourselves, others, and our world. Dr. Bach said flower remedies are like beautiful music or anything uplifting that raises our vibration and brings us nearer to our souls, helping us feel more at peace and giving us relief from our sufferings.

For example, if a client comes in with *extreme* negativity—jealousy, spite, hatred—to complement my coaching, I might offer the Bach flower remedy holly, which helps transform negative emotions into their polar opposites. With the right approach, holly can help transform hatred into love. I've gone through *bucketloads* of it in my life, and I can personally vouch for its effectiveness.

Holistic coaching is about knowing what to use and when. Some clients simply need reassurance and motivation to keep them moving toward their goals. Others have significant mental barriers we must first dismantle before they can move forward.

BREAKING DOWN BARRIERS

When Sarah first approached me for coaching, she was stuck both personally and professionally. Despite her ambitious goals, self-doubt, fear of failure, and limiting beliefs were holding her back. Through Mars Venus coaching, we worked on balancing her masculine energy (decisiveness and action) with her feminine energy (intuition and self-compassion), helping her break through these barriers.

Eliminating Personal Blocks

Together, we identified Sarah's internal fears and blocks. By shifting her mindset, she took bold steps toward her goals—goals she once thought were out of reach. With newfound clarity and confidence, Sarah embraced new opportunities and overcame the fears that had once limited her.

Empowering Leadership and Team Support

Sarah's personal breakthrough also transformed her leadership approach. She learned how to empower her team, supporting them in overcoming their own hurdles. With a focus on trust, empowerment, and mutual growth, she saw a significant improvement in team morale and productivity.

Enhanced Communication and Collaboration

Before coaching, communication barriers in her team often stalled progress. By understanding masculine and feminine energy dynamics, Sarah became more empathetic and a clearer communicator, leading to smoother collaboration and stronger team cohesion.

Achieving Goals with Confidence

With the tools I provided, Sarah aligned her goals with her deeper values. She now approaches both professional and personal challenges with a balanced mindset, combining assertiveness with intuitive reflection.

Improved Decision-Making and Work-Life Balance

Sarah's decision-making became more strategic, and she achieved a healthier work-life balance, avoiding burnout while maintaining productivity and fulfillment.

A key aspect of coaching my clients, including Glen and Sarah, to achieve their goals is testing and measuring, which allows them to see where they are on their coaching journey, while holding them accountable for their progress and keeping them motivated. I also bring a sense of humor to our sessions. I can't recall a single session where my client and I didn't share a good laugh.

> **Humor helps create a comfortable, open space for transformation, making the coaching journey both insightful and enjoyable.**

Emerging neuroscience indicates that effective coaching actively rewires the brain.[20] When I help clients break through limiting beliefs, the experience can trigger neuroplastic changes that reinforce adaptive thinking and resilience. In essence, coaching can build new neural pathways that enhance our ability to cope with challenges and seize growth opportunities.

Through consistent support, encouragement, and real-life success stories, I show clients that change is not only possible but also rewarding. As they embrace change, they gain confidence, improve their relationships, and experience greater success in life. In the end, overcoming fear of change is a journey, but with the right tools and mindset, it leads to lasting transformation and a more fulfilling life.

Witnessing the incredible transformation my clients

experience in such a short time impacts me greatly. Within just a few months, their lives dramatically change for the better. Their health improves; their relationships with partners, children, and colleagues strengthen, and, most importantly, their connection with themselves deepens. Seeing their self-confidence grow is truly inspiring. It's an honor to play a role in their growth and witness their *incredible evolution*.

THE SCIENCE OF SUCCESS: THE ROLE OF GRIT AND PERSEVERANCE

As I've found time and time again with my coaching clients, success isn't the result of luck. It's the result of *grit*.

Dr. Angela Duckworth has conducted groundbreaking studies on grit—the unique blend of passion and perseverance that drives people to pursue long-term goals, even in the face of tough challenges. In her research across a variety of fields, from education to business, Duckworth found that grit—not talent or intelligence—is the most consistent predictor of success.[21] Grit helps individuals maintain momentum, learn from failures, and push through obstacles. It's about the capacity to keep going when the going gets tough. Duckworth's findings suggest that individuals who are willing to put in sustained effort over time, despite setbacks, are more likely to reach their desired outcomes, emphasizing the importance of resilience, effort, and sustained *commitment*.

The grit concept aligns perfectly with my coaching approach.

The ability to build emotional resilience—to process setbacks and stay emotionally balanced—is an essential part of grit. Emotional resilience helps clients manage stress, overcome emotional blocks, and develop a sense of inner strength that enables them to keep moving forward.

Moreover, understanding the gender differences in emotional resilience can make developing grit even more powerful. For men, the drive for challenge and achievement is often linked to their need for independence and strength, so tapping into that masculine energy can bolster their perseverance. On the other hand, for women, emotional connection and support play a vital role in nurturing their resilience. Helping women develop grit involves not only reinforcing their commitment to long-term achievements but also encouraging them to seek the emotional support they need to thrive. By fostering grit through emotional resilience and gender intelligence, individuals can better navigate the challenges of life and relationships, ultimately achieving greater success.

IT ALL STARTED WITH A VISION

As well as offering coaching, I also teach meditation. If every client wanted to learn to meditate, it would be great for them. It would change their lives. But I know it's not for everyone, so I mostly keep meditation separate from my coaching practice.

I've been meditating for almost 50 years now. At age 15, I had a vision of what I can only describe as Christ or the

Holy Spirit—and that's coming from someone who wasn't religious in the slightest. I'd been feeling depressed for around six weeks, and I couldn't seem to shake the black fog around me. One day, while sitting at a coffee shop with a friend, I noticed a large charcoal drawing of an unborn fetus hanging on the wall. I had been oil painting since age 14, already on my way to becoming an artist, and the drawing caught my attention. I instinctively disliked the image—dark, with a lot of jagged edges—and staring at it made me feel worse. *Why did I dislike the drawing so much?* Where did that unsettling feeling come from? As I considered my unconscious reaction to the drawing, I realized I wasn't just seeing the image of an unborn fetus—I was seeing *myself* in that image. It was reflecting my own essence and pain back at me. In that moment, I understood myself at a deeper level.

Suddenly, a white-bearded man in flowing robes appeared before me. He didn't say he was Jesus—he could've been anyone—but whoever he was, I felt that he had come to bless me for daring to face myself in the mirror. A beautiful, warm feeling spread through my being. That feeling remained for around six weeks. Like I said, I wasn't religious—I didn't know what to make of the event—but to me the vision was undeniable, and once the feeling wore off, I wanted to recapture it somehow. That's when I began exploring meditation.

In the 70s, meditation wasn't the buzzword it is now. No one I knew meditated—I'd learned about the concept from listening to the Moody Blues—so finding someone to teach me even the basics wasn't easy. Searching through the phone book, I found a number for a transcendental meditation center. However, when I called, they informed me that the cost of learning to meditate would be $500, which for a kid in the 70s was a huge amount of money, so I was forced to abandon the idea.

It wasn't until age 20 that I finally learned to meditate from Guru Maharaji, who now goes by Prem—and it changed my life. Many years after hitting that initial financial barrier, I also learned transcendental meditation, and the practice resonated with me. I've now developed my own style—Sky Heart Meditation—and I offer to teach the basics to anyone who's interested. I still recall the disappointment I felt at meeting that insurmountable financial obstacle all those years ago, and I don't believe money should be a barrier to positive transformation. We should all have access to the tools we need to be successful in this life, whatever success looks like to the individual.

Unlock Inner Peace and Transform Your Life—a Free Gift with Coaching

After a lifetime immersed in meditation, I've come to believe that this simple yet powerful practice is one of the greatest gifts we can give ourselves. Meditation is effortless, profoundly healing, and proven to boost emotional resilience and mental clarity, and reduce stress. That's why I'm offering to teach this life-enhancing practice for FREE to every new client who commits to a four-month Mars Venus Coaching journey with me. This is more than just an offer—it's an invitation to take charge of your well-being and start living the extraordinary life you deserve. *Why wait?* Now's the perfect moment to step into clarity, balance, and growth. Let's begin your transformation today.

"Real transformation begins when we stop fighting our resistance and start understanding it. Gender-intelligent coaching helps people move forward not by pushing harder, but by aligning with their true emotional needs."

DR. JOHN GRAY

EMBRACE YOUR AUTHENTIC ENERGY

STACY HAVLICEK

Stacy Havlicek is a transformative life coach dedicated to empowering individuals to unlock their fullest potential with confidence and self-acceptance. From a young age, she has guided others to confront their challenges with clarity and courage, leveraging her warm demeanor, sharp insight, and authentic care. Her ability to create a safe, nonjudgmental space allows clients to explore their obstacles rationally and objectively, fostering profound personal and professional growth.

Before embarking on her coaching journey, Stacy built a

remarkable career in the energy industry, rising to the C-suite and eventually founding her own successful energy marketing firm. This achievement not only showcased her strategic acumen but also granted her the financial freedom to pursue her true passion: working with human and emotional energy.

Today, drawing on her unique blend of corporate expertise and holistic practices, Stacy helps clients clear emotional blocks, align their energy, and achieve their most ambitious goals. Her diverse clientele spans Disney interns and international diplomats, a testament to her versatility and impact. Stacy's approach integrates her extensive education and certifications, ensuring a well-rounded, evidence-based practice. She holds a Bachelor of Arts in chemistry from the University of Pennsylvania and a Master of Business Administration from Emory University, complemented by her participation in the Women's Forum of Harvard Business School. Stacy is also a certified energy risk professional, yoga instructor, yin yoga instructor, and practitioner of sound healing, Transcendental Meditation (TM), and Integrated Energy Therapy. These qualifications enable her to offer a holistic coaching experience that addresses both the mind and spirit.

With a deep commitment to helping others thrive, Stacy empowers her clients to navigate life's complexities with resilience and purpose. Her mission is to guide individuals toward a life of balance, fulfillment, and success, harnessing the same energy and determination that defined her own remarkable journey.

CAUGHT IN A CULTURAL SHIFT

I grew up in the 1970s across the river from New York City, raised by a fierce single mom who taught me a powerful lesson: "Get a good education and never rely on a man for anything." With little male influence in my life, I embraced the era's empowering message that women could do anything men could do. I thrived, graduating as salutatorian in high school, where I balanced my love for math and science with cheerleading and participating in the math team—no one ever told me those passions were "weird" for a girl. At the University of Pennsylvania, I majored in chemistry, confidently navigating male-dominated classes alongside other brilliant women, where mutual respect trumped gender norms.

But when I entered the workforce, everything changed. Starting my career in the energy sector in the Midwest, then moving to Texas and the South, I faced unexpected questions at just 25:

"Why such an analytical job?"

"Why work with so many men?"

"Why not dress more like a woman?"

"Aren't you afraid of becoming an old maid?"

Suddenly, gender became a lens I couldn't ignore. I didn't realize I was at the forefront of a cultural shift, challenging norms and sparking conversations that would grow from women in the workplace to the changing roles of men at home, and eventually to broader gender identity dialogues.

Over the past 25 years, I've immersed myself in understanding gender dynamics, drawing from the works of John Gray and Louann Brizendine, M.D., author of *The Female Brain* and *The Male Brain*. I celebrate the beautifully complementary differences between men and women, recognizing that misunderstandings often fuel conflict.

> **I firmly believe that communication and understanding can solve any problem, and I've made it my life's mission to share gender intelligence knowledge, helping people live happier, more connected lives.**

I've seen how understanding the complementary nature of masculine and feminine energies can heal misunderstandings. When we celebrate our differences instead of fighting them, we unlock deeper connection and harmony. I've seen single insights spark life-changing revelations, and in today's climate of gender confusion and tension, I'm passionate about guiding individuals, relationships, and the world toward healing through wisdom and empathy.

MY SEARCH FOR THE PERFECT FIT

In late 2020, as the world began to bloom again post pandemic, I joyfully embarked on a new adventure, settling into the vibrant heart of Jersey City. My business had just sold—a thrilling milestone—and I was surrounded by an incredible circle of dynamic Gen X women, all of us successful, independent professionals living our best lives across the river from New York City. I was in peak health, radiating energy, and savoring every moment of this exciting new chapter. Yet, amid all the abundance, I felt a gentle nudge in my heart—I was ready to welcome a meaningful romantic relationship into my life.

My fabulous friends and I dove into the modern dating scene, exploring online apps with curiosity and laughter, swapping stories and tips over coffee. That's when I stumbled upon John Gray's YouTube videos, a serendipitous discovery that lit up my journey. Learning that John had been the longtime assistant to Maharishi Mahesh Yogi—whose teachings I cherished through my yoga and TM (Transcendental Meditation) practices—opened my mind to his wisdom. I devoured hours of his content (often at double speed!), captivated by his insights on the differences between men and women. His take on how NYC women often lean into their masculine energy spoke directly to me, as if he'd peeked into my soul.

Twenty-five years earlier, I'd skimmed John's bestselling book, but back then I was a career-driven young woman, too focused on ambition to fully grasp its depth. Now, nearing my 50th birthday, with a trail of unfulfilling relationships behind me, I was ready to dive in with intention. I absorbed every lesson: love myself (check!), know my worth (check!), embrace my gifts (check!), and step into my feminine energy (a delightful work in progress!). I dated nonexclusively, letting men take the lead on planning—new territory for me, but I adapted with a smile, thanking them for their efforts. My amazing friends and a full, happy life kept me grounded, while I stayed emotionally unattached in the early stages, confidently moving forward. In a metro area of over 8 million, I knew my person was out there—and I was determined to find him.

And find him I did! By the time you read this, we'll be happily married, a success I credit in large part to John Gray's teachings. We read his books to each other, growing closer as we sharpened our relationship skills. My husband saw my passion for helping others and encouraged me to become a Mars Venus Coach—a perfect fit, as I've spent my life guiding both men and women toward self-love, partnership, and the love they long for. I've walked this path myself, and it's my calling to lead others on the same journey with warmth, wisdom, and a sprinkle of fun!

BALANCING FEMININE AND MASCULINE ENERGY

Coaching came naturally to me. I've been through the fire, painfully dragging myself forward on my knees. With tools and knowledge, I now help others on their journey so they can avoid fumbling in the darkness. I take a holistic approach to coaching, blending the Mars Venus methodology with energy work, meditation, and a deep understanding of gender dynamics—all rooted in my own transformative journey.

One of the biggest challenges I face is helping clients unlearn deeply ingrained patterns, especially around gender roles and self-worth. Many come to me with societal conditioning—like the "never rely on a man" mantra I grew up with—that can block them from embracing their authentic energy. It's tough to shift those mindsets, especially when clients are initially resistant to concepts like leaning into their feminine energy or letting go of control in relationships. I overcome this by meeting them where they are, using my own story to build trust. I share how I, too, had to relearn these dynamics after years of focusing on career over connection. My energy work and meditation techniques also help; I guide clients through practices like visualization and sound healing to release resistance and open their minds.

When Tabitha first came to me, she was a whirlwind of chaos—a 38-year-old graphic designer who'd been single for years and was convinced she'd "scare off every man in Jersey City," if she could even find one who met her impossibly high standards. She burst into our first session, latte in hand, declaring, "Stacy, I'm a hot mess! I'm too loud, too bossy, and my dating profile says I'm 'low-maintenance'—I'm basically lying to the internet!" I couldn't help but laugh—her energy was electric, if a bit scattered.

As a Mars Venus coach with personal experience, I knew that Tabitha's "bossy" vibe was her masculine energy in overdrive—a common trait for driven women in high-octane cities.

Side note: I've been called "bossy" for as long as I can remember, and I can remember learning to walk! Back then, a woman being "bossy" was considered negative, but I love that we've flipped it to "Lady Boss," with the positive meaning of a confident woman standing in her power.

Drawing on John Gray's teachings, I explained to Tabitha how she could balance her masculine and feminine energies to attract the kind of partner she craved. But she wasn't just about dating—she wanted to feel grounded, period. That's where my energy work and meditation techniques came in.

We started with a simple meditation to clear her blocks. I had her visualize her stress as a giant, glittery disco ball (her idea—she said it matched her personality). As she breathed deeply, I guided her to "dim the disco ball" with each exhale, using sound healing tones from my crystal bowls to amplify the calm. Tabitha giggled through the first session, muttering, "I feel like I'm in a spa for my soul!" But by the third, she was hooked, reporting she'd slept better than she had in years.

Next, we tackled her dating approach. I taught her to lean into her feminine energy—letting men plan dates while she focused on receiving with gratitude. At first, she balked: "Stacy, I can't just sit back—I'll plan the whole date in my head anyway!" But after a hilarious flop of a date where she accidentally took over and booked a paint and sip for a guy who hated art, she surrendered to the process. I had her journal her "feminine goddess" qualities daily, paired with energy-clearing exercises to release her need for control.

Six months later, Tabitha was a new woman. She'd met a sweet architect named Leo at a friend's barbecue—her first date where she didn't plan a thing. She showed up, radiant and relaxed, while standing in her power, and let him take the lead. They hit it off, and by their third date, he told her, "You're the most vibrant woman I've ever met, and I just feel good around you."

Tabitha called me, laughing through tears: "Stacy, I'm a goddess now—and I didn't even have to fake it!"

Beyond dating, Tabitha's whole life shifted. Her newfound calm from meditation helped her land a dream client at work, and she started hosting "energy reset" nights for her friends, proudly showing off her "Stacy techniques." Tabitha's transformation was a testament to the magic of Mars Venus coaching, blended with energy work and meditation—a perfect recipe for love, balance, and a good laugh along the way.

LIFT YOUR SPIRITS WITH MOVEMENT

As a Mars Venus coach with a focus on holistic well-being, I've seen how movement, like dancing, can be a powerful tool for emotional healing, and the science backs this up in some fascinating ways.

One compelling piece of research comes from a 2024 systematic review and meta-analysis, which found that dance interventions significantly reduce depression symptoms in older adults. The study, involving 508 participants across 19 randomized trials, showed a statistically significant decrease in depressive symptoms for those who danced compared to those who didn't engage in any intervention. The dance sessions ranged from 5 weeks to 18 months, and the results held true across various styles, suggesting that dancing's benefits aren't tied to a specific genre but rather the act of moving rhythmically itself.[22]

Another study, a 2021 meta-analysis of 28 randomized controlled trials with 2,249 participants, found that dancing for at least 150 minutes per week reduced depression symptoms, stress, and anxiety in adults, both with and without musculoskeletal disorders. The research highlighted that dancing triggers the release of endorphins—those feel-good chemicals in your brain—while also fostering mindfulness, which helps pull people out of negative thought loops often associated with depression.[23] This aligns with what I teach in my coaching: movement can ground you in the present, offering a break from rumination.

Dancing also has unique social benefits. A 2024 review pointed out that group dancing, especially with synchronized movements, promotes social bonding by releasing endorphins, which can further alleviate depressive symptoms.[24] This resonates with my energy work approach—connection, whether to yourself or others, is key to emotional balance.

From my perspective, dancing isn't just about the physical act—it's a way to tap into your emotional energy, release blocks, and reconnect with joy. I've seen clients, like Tabitha, transform their outlook through movement, and the science explains how: dancing combines physical activity, emotional expression, and social connection in a way few other activities do. It's a beautiful, accessible tool for anyone looking to lift their spirits.

SELF-LOVE—THE SECRET TO SUCCESS

As Tabitha and I demonstrate, the secret to love is embracing your authentic energy. For me, learning to step into my feminine goddess energy opened the door to meeting my husband. For Tabitha, it attracted a man who adored and appreciated her—the *real* her. When you love yourself and embody your true essence, you attract a partner who cherishes you for exactly who you are. At the end of the day, if we don't love ourselves, how can we expect another to love us?

Self-love is the key to success. When you value yourself, you set boundaries, take risks, and attract opportunities that align with your true purpose. Through coaching, it becomes clear that walking people back to themselves is the solution to most problems, including business issues. If loving oneself seems like an impossible goal (as it was for me before I started my healing journey), we coach to secondary or tertiary goals, which eventually strengthen self-love, acceptance, and understanding. I call it the "sneaky leaks" method. While we're not officially coaching to self-love, we're finding it anyway! Alternatively, we can directly coach to self-love, which is the faster route. When we pursue this path, most clients find that their other problems magically fix themselves. I love magic!

When we embrace self-love, we build more authentic connections, and as someone who rose to the C-suite in the energy industry and later ran a successful marketing firm, I can say that *authentic connection* is the secret to thriving in business.

That's right—success isn't just about strategy; it's about building genuine relationships with your team, clients, and partners. When people feel seen and valued, they'll go the extra mile, and that's what fuels growth. That's what fuels *success*.

> "We all have masculine and feminine energies within us. The key is learning when to lead with one and when to restore the other—especially in today's fast-paced, high-stress world."
>
> **DR. JOHN GRAY**

TRUTH LIES BENEATH THE SURFACE

ERIC LANTHIER

After the passing of his first wife, Eric Lanthier chose to specialize in the dynamics between men and women. Drawing from his experience in education, nonprofit leadership, and board governance, he earned a master's degree in education, a certificate in communication, and professional accreditations in both personal and organizational coaching.

Eric's unique background allows him to offer concrete, results-driven strategies to enhance clients' romantic, family, and professional relationships. As a relationship development coach, he helps men and women boost their emotional intelligence and resolve relational challenges with clarity and confidence.

RELATIONSHIPS NOURISHED BY EMOTIONAL WISDOM

In my decades of coaching, I've learned to look beneath the surface. As humans, we're oceans of emotion, lived experiences, and learned behaviors. Regardless of what's happening on the surface—whether it's a calm, choppy, or turbulent sea—there's always much more happening below. There's always more to the story.

In difficult situations, I use the principle of rereading, which allows me to see reality from another angle. For example, I once shared with my coach that I was experiencing relationship difficulties with a colleague. He replied, "If you try to see the problem from a different perspective, you'll understand the situation better." I admit that his answer frustrated me, but I agreed to play along. Thanks to his advice, I was able to see the situation for what it was. Instead of seeing my colleague's arrogance, I saw his fragility, his insecurity, his pain. From this experience, I learned to look beneath the surface of not just others' behavior but also my own, identifying *my need*, *my pain*, and *their emotion* (the perspective of the person who has challenged me). I'll explain further.

What If Our Conflicts Were Really About Our Needs?

Have you ever felt hurt because someone didn't listen to you, ignored your opinion, or interrupted you? Whether it's with your partner, at work, or among friends, those moments when you feel bad are often signals. Behind every strong emotion, there's usually an unmet need.

What's Really Behind Our Reactions?

When something bothers me, I can ask myself: *What would I have liked to experience instead? Did I need to be listened to, recognized, respected, or simply accepted as I am?*

In a relationship, for example, if my partner seems distant when I'm talking, I might feel a lack of attention or interest. It's not just that they aren't listening to me—it's that I feel invisible. At work, if a colleague ignores my idea, I might feel an unmet need for recognition, which can hurt, even if I don't realize why right away. What hurts even more is when this wound goes unnamed. That's when we can feel betrayed, rejected, or even humiliated.

What If I Could Turn This Pain into a Bridge to the Other Person?

What I'm experiencing is valid. When I put words to my pain,

I'm trying to walk with it and let it find a path toward connection. For example, if my partner often refuses my invitations to do things together, instead of sulking I can recognize that maybe I feel lonely or unimportant. Or if my boss criticizes me in front of everyone, I might feel humiliated. Identifying what I feel helps me avoid exploding or shutting down.

But what if I go even further? What if I try to see what the other person is experiencing too? Maybe they're also having a hard time. Maybe they feel stressed, tired, or insecure. My partner might be distant because they're exhausted or worried. My colleague who interrupts me might be trying to prove their worth, not put me down.

Name It, Understand It … and Build a More Authentic Connection

Next time I feel hurt in a relationship, I can:

1. Ask myself what need hasn't been met.
2. Name what I'm feeling with honesty and kindness.
3. Try to understand what the other person is experiencing.
4. Create a dialogue where both people can be heard.

That's how we move toward relationships that are more real, more human, more caring, and nourished by emotional wisdom. Only by exploring what lies beneath the surface can we truly understand anyone, including ourselves.

BELIEVE WHAT YOU PREACH, PRACTICE WHAT YOU TEACH

I had already been coaching and mentoring leaders for 35 years before I embarked on the Mars Venus coaching journey. After my wife Carole took her own life, missing her terribly, I decided that if I was going to rebuild my life, I wouldn't repeat the same mistakes I had made with her. I had to unblock myself emotionally and better understand the feminine universe, learning to look beneath the surface rather than taking everything at face value. That's when I reread *Mars and Venus on a Date*.

As I explored the Mars Venus philosophy, I realized I was missing certain tools and I had been coaching primarily by intuition. It was time to update my tool kit, and gender intelligence was exactly what I needed. Why?

Firstly, gender intelligence is based on science related to the brain and hormonal system. For example, neurological differences between genders influence leadership styles. Women tend to consult their teams more before making decisions, while men are perceived as more directive and performance-oriented.[25]

Additionally, one study found that higher testosterone levels are associated with lower risk aversion, especially in women. The study also establishes a link between testosterone and career choices, with higher levels linked to choosing riskier careers.[26] Essentially, high testosterone equals high levels of risk-taking, especially around finances.[27]

Studies also show that women are naturally more empathetic than men.[28] However, this strength isn't always valued in business. The science-based gender differences don't end there. For example, the brain's reward circuits are activated differently in men and women. In women, they're activated by prosocial behaviors, while in men they're activated by selfish behaviors.[29] It's important to note that these differences are general trends and significant individual variability exists. Furthermore, in the study of sex and gender differences, it's crucial to consider both biological and sociocultural factors.

Secondly, gender intelligence refines our emotional intelligence in four ways: it makes us more aware of ourselves and others, and it helps us identify and manage our emotions, which directly enhances our collaboration and communication skills.

1. Self-Awareness and Awareness of Others

- Understanding gendered emotional tendencies, allowing us to better recognize our own emotional tendencies and better understand the emotional reactions of others based on gender differences.
- Developing empathy by taking gendered perspectives into account, which encourages more nuanced and gender-sensitive communication.

2. Emotion Management
- Adapting emotional regulation strategies that consider gendered tendencies, helping to identify and overcome emotional blockages related to gender stereotypes.
- Providing tools to manage conflicts in a gender-sensitive way, fostering a more balanced approach to problem-solving.

3. Improved Teamwork
- Helping to create a more equitable and inclusive work environment by recognizing and valuing skills regardless of gender, which increases employee satisfaction and engagement, strengthens cohesion and collaboration within the team, and reduces biases and stereotypes.
- Stimulating creativity and innovation by leveraging gender diversity to enrich the creative process, encourage innovative thinking, and better anticipate the needs of a global market through a variety of perspectives.

4. Improved Leadership and Communication Skills
- Developing more empathetic and adapted communication skills.
- Effectively managing emotions and conflicts in a professional context.
- Promoting greater self-awareness, essential for effective leadership.

> **When we use gender intelligence to develop our emotional intelligence, we inspire others to desire our presence and perspective, enhancing every aspect of our lives.**

In summary, gender intelligence provides a framework for understanding, valuing, and using the differences between genders constructively, thereby improving personal and professional relationships, communication, leadership, and the work environment. It allows us to look deep beneath the surface, move beyond stereotypes, and foster better emotional understanding.

With the Mars Venus tools added to my tool kit, I was able to better understand the needs of those I coached. Gender intelligence also allowed me to avoid repeating the same mistakes with my second wife, Nathalie. At a conference, one of the attendees asked her what made me so special. She replied confidently, "What he teaches, he applies." It warmed my heart to hear that my wife sees that I practice what I preach.

MY GROWING CONCERN FOR MEN (AND WOMEN)

Overall, considering the biological differences between genders, I'm concerned about the emotional development of men.

> By developing emotional intelligence, we deepen relational bonds and improve our well-being. Our conversations become deeper, and our partners and children benefit too.

Unfortunately, however, men are less inclined than women to seek help, whether for physical, mental, or relational issues. They wait until it hurts, and often it's too late, or at least the path to healing is more laborious.

According to available data, women in Canada consult health care professionals more often than men. Here's an overview of the main differences …

In 2013 and 2014, 80.7 percent of women aged 12 and over reported having access to a regular doctor, compared to 68.9 percent of men. The difference is particularly marked in certain age groups, with only 46.6 percent of men aged 20 to 34 regularly accessing a doctor compared to 67.5 percent of women in the same age range.[30] Furthermore, women aged 25 to 54 are twice as likely as men to have consulted with a doctor in the past 12 months, with 10.8 percent consulting 12 or more times throughout the year compared to 4.6 percent of men.[31] The numbers paint a picture of men struggling to ask for help.

With all that said, women aren't immune to health struggles, especially when it comes to mental health. Surprisingly, Canada ranks 86 out of 116 countries for women's mental health, suggesting significant shortcomings in this area.[32]

Considering the increasing challenges modern men and women face, understanding gender intelligence, thereby increasing emotional intelligence, is more important than ever.

When I explain to my wife that I once had a very low score in emotional intelligence, she says she feels like I'm talking about another man. By studying and applying gender intelligence—and through trials, accompaniment, community, and faith in a relational and inspiring God—it's almost as if I have become another man.

MARS VENUS—A TRANSFORMATIONAL APPROACH TO COACHING

While I'm proud of my own emotional unblocking, I'm also proud of my clients who have worked hard to develop their own emotional intelligence.

I'll always remember one introverted client who was unable to express what he felt. He couldn't smile or express to his wife how good she made him feel. After a few sessions with me, he was able to identify character traits through his wife's actions. Concretely, instead of complimenting her on *what* she was doing, he was able to say to her, "Darling, I can see your generosity through your listening and your giving of yourself." He told me, "The more I see her for who she is, the more I experience harmony, and it fills me with happiness, especially when I express her character traits to her. It opens me up." Learning and applying gender intelligence was the key to his transformation.

Since becoming a Mars Venus coach, my coaching style and vision of couple life and leadership have changed. I now:
- Talk less, listen more, and ask more questions.
- Tend to give fewer solutions and better understand the emotion that hides beneath the surface of what people are expressing.
- Feel less responsible for the unhappiness of others, seeing my role differently. I now see it more as providing an ear that relieves the person in front of me because they can express themself to someone who doesn't judge them for what they have or haven't done. Instead, I'm there to welcome, understand, and offer empathy in the face of their pain.

Sometimes, I don't know what to say to a client. When this happens, I ask them questions, rephrase what they've said, validate the emotion they're expressing, or ask them to clarify their thoughts or feelings. Once I understand the situation, using gender intelligence, I decide how to proceed. For example, if I'm coaching a man, I might ask, "What do you intend to do?" Or, "If you were advising a friend in the same situation, what would you tell them?" If I'm coaching a woman, I might ask, "What has helped you in similar situations in the past?" And, "What's different between what you experienced then and what you're experiencing now?"

The more I listen rather than immediately offering solutions, the more I understand what they're experiencing, and the better I'm able to identify their needs. Revealing what truly lies beneath the surface requires a combination of listening and questioning. To paraphrase a wise king of antiquity, he who listens obtains the ability to advise well.

AN EMOTIONALLY INTELLIGENT APPROACH TO LIFE

By applying gender intelligence to every aspect of our lives, we *enhance* every aspect of our lives. I know it, because I've experienced it. Here's how I've applied gender intelligence and emotional intelligence to business, coaching, relationships, love, and life in general.

Business

In business, people don't just buy your products or services. It's you they choose. The secret is to understand what motivates a leader to change. The better we feel about ourselves, the more we can connect with our employees, our colleagues, our clients, and our partners.

As soon as the person I'm collaborating with unblocks emotionally and relationally, they multiply their influence and ability to communicate their vision.

Relationships

I accompany the people I collaborate with to identify the emotion behind a communication and the character trait that hides behind an action.

For example, when a man is offended by the fact that his wife told him he works too much and doesn't spend enough time with her, I ask him to identify the emotion that hides behind her statement. He ends up understanding that she misses him, which gives him a new, more empathetic perspective.

Regarding character traits, I ask him to identify the identity behind the gesture. For example, instead of telling his partner that the painting she created on the canvas is beautiful, he says to her, "Wow darling, this painting highlights your creativity!" This approach was developed by the organization Character First helps to enhance our relationships.

Identifying the emotion behind an action allows us to express that we care about the other person's state of mind, and the character trait allows us to make our partners feel seen and understood.

Love

When something my wife says or does frustrates me, I turn to three principles:

1. Anger hides its guests.
2. Lower the tone.
3. The BAG principle.

Anger Hides Its Guests

As John Gray teaches so well, behind anger often hides sadness, fear, disappointment, and regret. When I feel the emotional tension rising within, the little hamster in my head tries to understand the source of this anger or frustration, which leads me to reconnect with my partner's pain.

Lower the Tone

When I connect with the guests hidden behind the anger and I'm in connection with the person I'm interacting with (my wife), I'm able to lower the tone and enter into emotional connection mode instead of being in emotional destruction mode, which brings a change of atmosphere. Then I approach my wife and touch her hand or arm to show her I want to connect.

The BAG Principle

The BAG principle highlights three interaction types, namely generating *buzz*, *anticipation*, and *gratitude*.

The *buzz* is produced by a small surprise, either through an unexpected service, a touching word, or an affectionate gesture. For example, if I buy my wife a small gift, such as her favorite chocolate or flower, outside of a special occasion, it shows that I appreciate her, which activates her oxytocin.

Anticipation is produced by planning a romantic outing for your partner so she has a joy to cling to and share with her loved ones, creating a wave of happiness.

Gratitude is generated by an intellectual, emotional, or physical connection. The intellectual connection is a starting point to arrive at the emotional connection. It begins by you being interested in what your partner says. Every time you show interest, you build admiration and gratitude in her.

The emotional connection forms when you seek to see and understand your partner's emotional experience by listening with empathy and without judgment. To transition from an intellectual connection to an emotional connection, ask the following questions:

"How did you feel in this circumstance?"

"What did it make you experience?"

"What pain did it cause? I imagine it made you joyful, sad, anxious, disappointed, guilty (depending on the case)."

The physical connection forms through an affectionate "nonsexual" touch, such as a caress, a hug, taking your partner's hand, or even putting on romantic music and dancing with her. These approaches generate gratitude in women, and gratitude fuels our spouses' emotional imagination and nourishes our desire to repeat the behavior.

Life

My coach, Richard Bernstein, and one of my colleagues, Normand Joseph, a speaker trainer, taught me that humility is the key to success in life. At the coaching level, Richard often shares his shortcomings and reminds me that doing so helps people open up. He's an example I strive to imitate.

Normand takes the same approach with his workshops. One day, he said to me, "Eric, don't talk about your successes, talk about your failures so people feel that you understand them.

However, when you talk about others, talk about their successes so they see that you're seeking to honor them." Humility is a tool for success in life, as it makes the people I collaborate with feel comfortable and connected. I like to remind myself, day after day, that it's not my successes, achievements, or trophies that make me a potentially inspiring person. It's what I've learned from my shortcomings, my pain, my failures, and the mistakes I've made. Those are the lessons that inspire the people around me.

In closing, never forget—there's no growth without turbulence, and to survive the turbulent times, we could all use some coaching.

> "Understanding emotions is the master key to unlocking behavior. Men and women may express their emotions differently, but when we learn to look beyond words and actions to the feelings beneath, real connection becomes possible."
>
> **DR. JOHN GRAY**

WHEN SCIENCE MEETS SOUL

PETRA FÜRST

Petra Fürst is the founder of Soulmate Coaching, a transformational relationship brand that helps women attract and build deeply fulfilling, soulmate-level love—no matter their age or past experiences. Her work combines powerful tools like NLP, hypnosis, gender intelligence, and her signature Happy Relationship Now methodology to create lasting inner shifts that lead to real, meaningful connection.

Petra's mission is to guide women back to their worth, their radiance, and their power so they can attract the kind of love that doesn't just feel good—it feels *right*.

GENDER INTELLIGENCE SAVED MY RELATIONSHIP

Gender intelligence became deeply important to me through a very personal experience in my own long-term relationship. After six years together, I started noticing a recurring conflict that caused growing tension between me and my partner. I love to talk, especially after a long day filled with work and parenting responsibilities. In the evenings, I would sit down with my partner, eager to connect, process the day, and share my thoughts. But the more I talked, the more distant he seemed. He grew quiet, withdrawn, and I began to feel hurt and rejected.

At first, I took it personally. I assumed he wasn't interested in me or what I had to say. This misunderstanding led to arguments, as I felt ignored and he felt overwhelmed. We started fighting about what, at the time, seemed like a communication issue but was actually something much deeper.

It wasn't until I discovered the concept of gender intelligence that everything shifted. Since exploring the Mars Venus methodology, research in the field of neuroscience and hormonal psychology, particularly around how testosterone and oxytocin influence our behavior in relationships, has shaped the way I coach. What many people don't know is that men and women regulate stress in completely different ways—and understanding this is *crucial* for creating happy, lasting love.

I learned that men often need quiet time to recharge, especially after a demanding day. They aren't distancing themselves emotionally; they're biologically wired to disconnect temporarily in order to restore their testosterone and regain their sense of clarity and focus, through rest, silence, or focusing on one thing at a time. That's why many men "retreat into their cave" after a long day. It's not rejection—it's biology.

Women, on the other hand, lower their stress through oxytocin, which is produced by *talking*, *sharing*, and *feeling connected*. That's why women often want to talk at the end of the day—to reconnect and regulate their emotions.

When we don't understand these differences, we can take things *personally*. She thinks he's distant or uninterested, and he feels pressured or overwhelmed. But once we integrate the science into our communication, everything shifts. We stop fighting biology and start *working with it*.

That's why gender intelligence is a pillar of everything we do at Soulmate Coaching. Because love isn't just an emotion—it's also a *biochemical dance*. And when we learn the steps, we finally create the connection we've always longed for.

Understanding this completely changed my perspective. I stopped taking my partner's silence personally and started giving him the space he needed. And what happened next was beautiful: When he felt recharged, he naturally came back with more energy, presence, and affection. Our connection grew stronger, not because we changed who we were, but because we finally understood each other.

Once I experienced powerful results in my own relationship, I felt a deep desire to integrate gender intelligence into my work. As the founder of Soulmate Coaching, I now use the Mars Venus methodology to enrich and deepen my coaching programs. While we already focus on understanding relationship dynamics and emotional needs, the Mars Venus framework adds another essential layer—one that brings clarity, compassion, and practical tools to help our clients build truly meaningful connections.

What I love most about the Mars Venus philosophy is it emphasizes the beauty of our differences. Instead of trying to make men and women the same, it teaches us how to understand one another more deeply and create fulfilling relationships based on mutual respect and appreciation. Understanding how men and women differ—not just emotionally but also hormonally and neurologically—can be life-changing.

For me, learning gender intelligence was truly eye-opening and helped me create more harmony and connection in my personal life. That's why the Mars Venus philosophy is so important to me—and why it's a foundational element of the work I do. When we understand how the male and female brain work, we stop misinterpreting one another; we prevent unnecessary fights, and we create space for true connection, love, and peace.

BECOME MAGNETIC!

At Soulmate Coaching, I don't just teach dating strategies or communication tools. I help my clients do the deep work—healing old wounds, breaking unconscious patterns, and returning to the truth of who they really are. My unique coaching approach uses a combination of deep emotional healing, structured transformation, and soulful energy work—all grounded in clear, science-based tools. I bring together the worlds of NLP, hypnosis, the Mars Venus philosophy, and our own Soulmate Relationship Now methodology to help my clients shift on every level: mind, heart, body, and energy.

But it's not just about the tools—it's also about how my team of certified Soulmate coaches and I hold space. Our clients often tell us they feel *deeply seen* and *safe* for the first time in their lives. We ask the uncomfortable questions others avoid. We listen to what's *not* being said. We challenge our clients lovingly but directly. And we guide them to embody the version of themselves that attracts a soulmate—not by chasing love, but by *becoming* love.

Frequently, our clients come in with years—or decades—of disappointment, heartbreak, or limiting beliefs. They don't believe in love anymore. They don't even believe in themselves. Our job in those moments is to believe *for* them until they can believe again. That's where the deep inner work begins.

One client experience that still touches my heart involves Anna, a 60-year-old retired teacher from Hamburg. She had never been married and secretly believed that love just wasn't meant for her.

At Soulmate Coaching, we work with the five inner child traumas: abandonment, constant criticism, emotional and physical abuse, overprotection (which leads to isolation), and parentification (loss of self). Through our hypnosis sessions with Anna, we uncovered a deep subconscious block rooted in her childhood—where she had learned that being loved meant being invisible and self-sacrificing. She had experienced loss of self and constant criticism. Anna grew up in a home where love was quiet, but pain was loud. Her mother was trapped in a deep, chronic depression—emotionally absent, unreachable, unable to care for herself, let alone her daughter. So Anna stepped in. As a little girl, she made her own school lunches. She brushed her teeth and put herself to bed at night. No one checked in. No one noticed.

Her father? Always angry. Always criticizing her mother, and eventually Anna too.

But under that anger was something deeper: helplessness. From the Mars Venus perspective, his rage wasn't really about Anna or even his wife. He was a man who felt powerless to make his partner happy. And instead of expressing his pain, he masked it with control, harshness, and blame.

In truth, Anna didn't grow up with caregivers. She grew up learning to survive emotional neglect and unspoken wounds. And she learned early on: *If I don't take care of it, no one will.* This led to her staying single her whole life. Even though she desired to get married and have a family, she was unconsciously frightened that she might end up in the same situation as her parents.

Her inner child's fear of pain was bigger than her adult's

desire for a relationship.

Anytime Anna got close to dating someone, she felt this deep uncontrollable panic and would retreat. *Relationships just aren't meant for me*, she told herself, focusing all her love on the children in her class. At work, she felt loved in a safe way; at home, she was lonely.

Together, we rewired that pattern and replaced it with a new belief: she could be fully seen *and* fully loved. Rewiring is deep work that takes weeks of personal coaching to achieve. The beautiful thing is, with the right technique and a commitment to growth, anything negative or destructive learned can be unlearned.

Two months later, Anna met Victor, a widower, at her local bookstore. They started talking about poetry and ended up sitting for hours, sharing stories and laughter. It was the first time in her life that she didn't feel panic when talking to an attractive man. Instead, she felt joy. Anna finally started to live the life she always dreamed of. When Victor proposed to her 7 months later, she cried tears of joy. She never thought she would find love, and now she was sharing life with her soulmate.

Anna recently wrote me a postcard that said, *It feels like my heart finally woke up after decades of sleep.*

At Soulmate Coaching, we often help our clients unlearn the idea that love has to be hard or they have to earn it, especially women who have spent their lives over-giving, over-functioning, waiting for crumbs of affection. I teach them to receive. To soften. To trust. To become magnetic—not through effort, but through alignment.

Sabine came to us feeling disillusioned and heartbroken after a 30-year marriage ended unexpectedly. She always felt responsible for everyone's feelings and needs, often feeling guilty without understanding why. This was the result of a childhood pattern: *I must give to others in order to be loved. Only if I perform, will I be good enough.*

In her marriage, she had given it all, kept a perfectly clean house after her long and demanding workday, raised their two children with love and dedication, and tried hard to be a good wife. She did everything for everyone, but nothing for herself.

Halfway through their marriage, her husband started to lose physical attraction to her. He respected her for her hard work, but he didn't admire or desire her anymore.

Sabine worked harder, went on a weight loss journey, changed her hair color, and even read a book about how to perform better in the bedroom. She fought for her relationship, but nothing worked.

It took another 15 years until they finally got divorced. Over 15 years of living with someone, feeling lonely and misunderstood.

Many clients wish they had come to us sooner. At age 56, Sabine didn't feel like she could start over again. She was tired, overwhelmed, and scared.

"What if I never find someone?"

"I'm too old, nobody will find me attractive!"

"All the good men are already married."

She expressed these fears, which are normal, during our onboarding call. Such thoughts are the unconscious mind trying to protect us from another failure, another heartbreak. But if we don't break through these fears, we'll never find love. If we believe these voices in our heads, we'll stay alone, complaining that there are no good men out there.

Alternatively, we can take a leap of faith and jump into the cold sea. After swimming for a few minutes, the water doesn't feel cold anymore; it starts to feel fine, and we wonder why we didn't jump in sooner.

For Sabine, the best chapter of her life lay ahead.

Her coaching journey started with inner work. Before we teach our clients dating skills and how to understand men, they first need to heal from past experiences and unprocessed heartbreak and disappointments. Only then are they ready to attract their soulmate. Using our Happy Relationship Now methodology—which combines deep emotional transformation with practical relationship tools from NLP, hypnosis, and gender intelligence—we helped her reconnect with her feminine energy, release years of limiting beliefs, and finally let go of the fear of being too old, too late, or too much.

During our first years of life, several factors combine to create our first relationship imprints: Were our needs met? Did we feel loved and safe? Were our caregivers there for us when we needed them? Did they encourage and support us? Did they give us the love we needed? Or did they not? Did they sometimes give us the love we needed and sometimes not? Our first love imprint forms our sense of self-worth. *What am I worth? Am I worth something to others?*

As mentioned, at Soulmate Coaching, we work with the five inner child traumas. Many people have more than one, and these traumas can cause them to repeat the same behaviors again and again. Why? Because the inner child hopes that by repeating certain patterns, it can one day create the happy ending to close the story. But there's no happy ending. Repeating the same patterns only creates more pain, again and again, with different partners.

In order to have a happy ending, we must change the pattern, not necessarily the partner.

Later in childhood, after we start interacting with our environment, learning to speak and interact with others, we unconsciously observe our parents' or caregivers' relationship patterns. How does the masculine treat the feminine? How does the feminine feel around the masculine? How are they communicating their needs and emotions to each other? How are they communicating feedback or concerns? This is our second love imprint, and it creates our own relationship behavior pattern. At Soulmate Coaching, we identify eight different relationship patterns, guiding our clients to a better understanding of themselves and their relationships.

After just a few months of working with us, Sabine had completely transformed her energy. She no longer showed up in dating from a place of fear or over-giving. She knew her value, set boundaries with love, and attracted a man who respected and adored her. They met at a cooking class in Tuscany—a trip she booked as part of her "new life" vision—and they've been together ever since. She says, "It's not just that I met him. It's that I was finally ready for him."

I'm not the kind of coach who just gives advice. I walk beside my clients as they transform. I see their highest potential, even when they've forgotten it. At Soulmate Coaching, we have a success guarantee. We work with our clients until they find love, no matter how long it takes. Some, like Anna, find it after three months; others, like Sabine, find it after six months. Everyone's journey is different.

THE BEAUTIFUL TRUTH ABOUT LOVE

We often think love is something we must *search for* or *chase*—as if it's outside of us, hiding somewhere, waiting to be discovered. Clients often ask: "Where do I find him?" But there's no specific location where you'll find your soulmate. If you're not ready, you won't find him, not even in a room of 1,000 people. If you're ready, you can meet him anywhere: at the dentist, the supermarket, while walking your dog. The truth is, love finds you when you're fully aligned with your worth, your truth, your energy, and your heart. Love doesn't come from finding the perfect person. Love comes from becoming the version of yourself that allows real love in.

Whether you're single or in a relationship, your journey to love begins with the most important relationship of all: the one you have with yourself.

The soulmate you're longing for isn't looking for your perfection; they're looking for your *authenticity*. Your presence. Your softness. Your joy. And most of all, your openness.

I've seen women fall in love at 55, 63, 71, not because they got lucky, but because they finally gave themselves permission to be seen, to be loved, to receive. That's the real secret: you don't attract love by doing more—you attract it by being more of *you*.

Once you stop trying to impress, fix yourself, or chase someone who doesn't choose you, the right person shows up. The one who sees you. Chooses you. And loves you, not in spite of who you are, but *because* of it.

EMBRACE THE AUTHENTIC YOU

One of the most important lessons I've learned—not just as a coach, but as a woman, a mother, and a human being—is: *no method, no science, and no relationship tool works if, deep down, you believe you're not enough.* Whether someone is single or in a relationship, we see this same pattern over and over again—the quiet, painful belief of, *I'm not enough.*

Not pretty enough. Not smart enough. Not successful enough.
Too much. Too emotional. Too needy.

Just ... not right the way I am.

This belief silently shapes how we show up in love, in business, and in life. It makes us shrink. It makes us hustle for approval. It makes us betray ourselves—just to be liked, chosen, or not abandoned.

So many of the women (and men) who come to us at Soulmate Coaching are incredibly accomplished. They've built careers. They've raised children. They've survived heartbreak, illness, betrayal, loss. On the outside, they're strong. But when we sit down and peel back the layers, a quieter voice emerges— one they've carried for years, sometimes a lifetime.

Maybe I'm just not lovable the way I am.

Maybe I always have to try harder.

If I really show who I am, I'll be too much. Or not enough.

This isn't something a simple mindset shift can fix. It's not about "thinking positively." It's deep. Often, it's rooted in childhood—the way we were treated, or not treated.

The love we had to earn.

The attention we only received when we performed, helped, achieved, pleased.

And so, we learned to abandon ourselves in order to be loved by others. But here's the truth I wish the whole world knew: *the more you abandon yourself, the further you move away from love.* Not just romantic love, but *real* love. The kind that sees you. Feels you. Chooses you. The kind of love you're truly craving.

That's why, even though at Soulmate Coaching we teach

science-backed tools like gender intelligence, NLP, and hypnosis, the real magic happens when we go deeper—into the subconscious patterns, the old childhood wounds, and the emotional blocks that say, *You have to be someone else to be loved.* It's not true.

**Healing begins the moment we stop performing
and start coming home to ourselves.**

Love begins the moment we stop asking, *How do I need to look and act to be loved?* and start asking, *Can I allow myself to be seen—as I truly am?* That's the deeper work. That's the truth behind lasting connection. And that's the journey I walk with every client—back to their own worthiness, their own authenticity, and ultimately the love that was never outside of them in the first place.

That's why, inside Soulmate Coaching, our deepest work isn't teaching women how to "get a man" or "fix their relationship." It's guiding them to *remember who they truly are*—before the world told them to shrink, to be nice, to be less. Even if the trauma started in early childhood, your soul knows who you really are. It always remembers and holds that truth for you.

Because only when you are fully YOU—in your power, in your softness, in your truth—can the right person find you. The one who says, "Yes. You. Just like that. Don't change a thing." And that's not a fairy tale.

That's what happens when *science meets soul*.

When *healing meets strategy.*
When *you finally come home to yourself.*

> "Self-development isn't about fixing ourselves—it's about rediscovering who we truly are beneath the conditioning and fear."
>
> **DR. JOHN GRAY**

UNLOCK EXCLUSIVE BONUS CONTENT!

Dr. John Gray and his certified coaches have created powerful resources to enhance your understanding of gender intelligence and the wider Mars Venus philosophy.

Inside your free bonus pack, you'll get:
- Audio downloads
- Printable worksheets
- Practical tools and resources—and more!

Visit marsvenuscoaching.com/bookbonus to access your bonuses now.

GENDER INTELLIGENCE

The Key to Business Success

RICH BERNSTEIN

Rich Bernstein is the president and CEO of Mars Venus Coaching and comes with a wealth of experience spanning over 25 years. He has owned and managed companies, both private and publicly traded, in various industries.

Rich has been active in the coaching industry since 2003 and has functioned as a support manager as well as a global sales director internationally. His background in sales, support, marketing, and business management makes him uniquely qualified to help licensees and business owners learn important strategies for business success. Rich has a full complement of skills and experience in marketing, sales processes, financial models, time management techniques, and team building.

FROM BURNED-OUT BUSINESS OWNER TO THRIVING BUSINESS COACH

Before I became a coach, I owned my own business. I was working day in and day out. I couldn't get home for dinner. I missed my kids' recitals and football games. I was missing so many important events in my family's lives. I finally decided enough was enough, and I sold the business.

Through my experience as a business owner, I learned what to do and, importantly, what not to do to become a success. I was continually thinking, *I have so much knowledge to share!* I'd really like to help other business owners escape the perpetual work week. This is when I decided to become a business coach.

Until that point, I had never heard the words business and coach in the same sentence. The first time I heard it, I thought, *Wow! That's a really good idea! I'd like to be a business coach.* Because I was a business owner, I knew what it was like to not make payroll, not be able to cash your own check, not get home for dinner, and to work 70 hours per week. Trust me, it's no way to live.

After a few years of business coaching, I met John Gray. When he asked me to join his team as a business coach utilizing the Mars Venus methods, including gender intelligence, the first question I asked was, "What does Mars Venus have to do with business?"

John's response? "Everything!"

If you don't think business and relationships work in sync with one another, you're greatly mistaken. Gender intelligence applies as much in business as it does in our personal lives. Your relationships with your clients, your customers, your employees, your vendors, and your suppliers—they're all integral to the success of a business.

GENDER INTELLIGENCE IS A NECESSITY IN BUSINESS

Realizing that relationships drive a business gave me a whole new perspective on business and success. When I first came to Mars Venus, I started to learn about gender intelligence. Gender intelligence describes how men and women think and process information differently, and the differences in how they talk, shop, and relate. As I gained more knowledge on the subject, I wondered ... *If men and women buy differently, are salesmen selling to them differently?*

With supervision and input from John Gray, I created a sales training based on gender intelligence. In that training, I educated students on John's theories, adding the idea that because men and women are wired differently, men and women must buy differently. The purpose was to teach salespeople to sell differently. In addition, I discussed how men and women, who process information differently, guide others and are inspired in different ways.

There's no "one-size-fits-all" approach to instructing and educating people. Both genders react differently. Men don't want all the details; they prefer to be told what needs to be done. Women would rather have more information about the "why" of an assignment. Women's brains are optimized to communicate better between the two hemispheres compared to men's.[33] Because the two hemispheres are more strongly connected, when you instruct women, you have to connect the instructions or end result with everything else in their lives. They need to understand the big picture—the why.

> **I've been doing gender-intelligent business coaching for over 17 years, and I can tell you there's no way to grow your company without keeping these points at the forefront of your mind: men and women are different and need different things in business and in life.**

Before I came to Mars Venus, I mainly focused on coaching in sales and marketing. However, the problem was, if all I taught were sales and marketing, the minute I left, the business began to fall apart. When you focus only on sales and marketing, with no concentration on creating and continuing relationships with clients, business plummets. When I used the Mars Venus methodologies, I put sales and marketing on a foundation of relationships, and the results came faster and were more sustainable. John taught me that you can teach business owners how to deliver relationship coaching to help their businesses grow. After all, sales and marketing are all about building a connection with your clients—which is very important to a business's success.

John Gray's philosophy on the differences between men and women should be integrated into the business world. I've seen, firsthand, the success businesses achieve when teaching leadership, sales, and customer service with the Mars Venus approach. Gender intelligence is the future of business.

CONFERENCE ROOM CONFUSION

Because men and women process information differently, we also work differently. For example, say there's a meeting going on. There are five men and five women sitting around a conference table, and the leader is standing up, conducting the meeting. There's an unspoken understanding between the men: if they have something to contribute, they'll speak up. They don't raise their hands; they don't wait to be called on; they just blurt it out. The leader knows this too. He doesn't call on them individually—"Hey, Bob, what do you think we should do?"—because he knows that will embarrass Bob. After all, if Bob has something to say, he'll let it be known.

Women, however, tend to view that method as unprofessional. They're actually waiting to be called on, as they believe this is how an effective, professional environment should run. The men believe that if she has something to say, she'll say it! So why call on her if she's not speaking up? This miscommunication (or lack of communication) causes women to feel like they're not being heard. By the end of the meeting, the women leave, thinking, *I can't believe he didn't ask me anything! He doesn't acknowledge me. He doesn't value me as a member of this team!* However, the man actually does value her—that's why he didn't call on her. Isn't that interesting?

There are so many similar situations happening in the corporate world today. If two men are standing by the water cooler discussing the game they watched over the weekend and a woman walks up, they stop talking. This leads her to feel left out or unincluded. However, the men feel as if they're doing her a service. They assume she doesn't care about the game, so why keep talking about it? Before you know it, there's discord and conflict between the men and women in the company, and the business suffers. This is why teaching gender intelligence to professionals in all work environments is so powerful.

I was with John once at a speaking engagement in Las Vegas for the Anti-Aging Conference. We were backstage with a stagehand who was prepping the mic for John. The stagehand had a walkie-talkie and was speaking with a woman up in the sound booth. She said to the stagehand, "Look, I want you to hook pack A on his belt and put the little lapel mic on his collar.

But I also—and I want you to understand that the last time we did this, one of the batteries went out, and so we had to switch right in the middle of the guy's talk—so what I prefer to do is to have pack B on the other side. Put that to his shirt so there are actually two of them. We'll need two mics. I might have one on, and I'm going to switch it over if something happens to the first line, and nobody will know the difference because you know this happened before …" She went on and on with a long explanation of what had to be done.

The stagehand looked at John and said, "I don't need to know all that. Just tell me to put the second mic on!"

John, being the authentic man he is, walked out on stage during his talk and told that story. "This is men and women," he explained. "She felt the need to explain why she wanted him to do something. However, the man just needed to know what needed to be done so he could do it. That's gender intelligence." The two genders need to be aware of the problems they cause one another by not communicating effectively and positively. Through Mars Venus coaching, men and women can change how they communicate with one another, speaking in the other's "language." We need to recognize and embrace our differences, and understand how they impact the opposite gender.

It's vital to understand that men and women will respond to your marketing practices differently. Men and women will respond to your sales process differently. When I ask business leaders if they believe that men and women buy differently, 90 percent say, "Of course they do."

Then I ask, "Knowing that, do you train your salespeople to sell differently?"

Dead silence.

Then I ask, "What about your leadership styles? Do you lead men and women differently?"

Dead silence.

If a person truly believes and accepts that men and women are different—which they are—how can they not use gender intelligence to help build their business and create a flourishing company?

Many people have said to me, "Rich, isn't that a bit manipulative?"

I always give the same example. When I was a little kid, I learned how to "talk" to horses from an old cowboy. He told me, "You know, horses are prey in the wild. We're the predators. Horses will be naturally skeptical of you and your intentions. If you walk up to the horse with your palms open and out, and walk toward them, they'll run away. But if you close your hands in a fist and place them by your sides, they'll run toward you." Is that manipulation? No. It's just being a better communicator. Using gender intelligence to better guide the men and women on your team is being a better communicator. It's speaking their language.

YOU MANAGEMENT, NOT TIME MANAGEMENT

Mars Venus Coaching is very special to me because I want to prevent business owners from uttering the words I found myself saying constantly: "Please record the kid's (insert extracurricular activity here) because I won't be there to see it." It killed me to have to say that. I don't want others to go through what I went through.

I've been to countless companies and asked the owners how many hours they've been working, and they sigh and say, "Eighty? Maybe ninety?" That used to be me. I know what it's like, and I really want to help those people.

One way to get out of that cycle of perpetually missing out on life's events is effectively managing time. And, like everything else, men and women manage time very differently. Everyone gets 24 hours per day, whether you like it or not. So, technically speaking, you can't manage time. The only thing you can manage is you. What you do in this minute, what you do in this hour are choices you make. Men and women approach time management very differently, and it's important to learn how to manage yourself around time in the most productive way.

Being aware of what you do and how you do it is the first step. Taking action is the next. Coaching is all about taking action and showing a client they can flourish. Yes, it's partly about gaining new knowledge, but there's more to it. Many people say, "Knowledge is power!"

> **I don't believe that knowledge is power. I believe you have to implement it to make it powerful.**

It's kind of like the potential energy a rock has sitting on top of a hill. It doesn't have any energy until it starts to roll down the hill.

ALL COACHING IS NOT CREATED EQUAL

When I first came to Mars Venus Coaching, I felt like I had finally "seen the light," so to speak. Until then, my business coaching hadn't focused on leading, coaching, and interacting with clients using gender intelligence. Now I see it's the only way to achieve maximum success both in business and in our everyday relationships.

The three parts of coaching are clarity, planning, and accountability. Each part looks very different to men and women. For example, once when I was coaching a couple, the wife stated she wanted to feel more supported by her husband. This was a cause of much conflict in their marriage. I asked the wife, "What does support look like to you?"

She thought for a moment and said, "Well, I'd like him to find me in the house when he comes home and give me a hug and tell me that everything's going to be OK so I don't feel alone."

Then I asked the husband, "Do you support your wife?"

"Of course!" he said.

"What does support look like to you?"

"I go to work every day," he replied. "I pay the bills. I make sure she has a home, money for groceries, and a car. That's support."

Men and women see things very differently and can have very different perspectives on the same word—in this case, support. Gaining clarity by understanding each other's perspective is the first step. Creating a plan comes next. You can understand that your wife needs to feel supported, but if you keep doing what you've been doing, the relationship won't flourish. Instead, it will stagnate and brew resentment.

For example, if a wife has a problem and wants to feel supported, she may go to her husband and tell him what's happening. She goes into the conversation simply wanting to vent her frustration and hear encouraging words. However, nine times out of ten, the husband starts listing off ways to fix her problem. Why? Because fixing what's wrong makes him feel like he's supporting her. Except he isn't—at least not in the way she needs. His wife needs to be heard. "Tell me more," the husband should say. Or, "That's awful! I'm sorry. That must feel terrible for you." Then the wife feels heard and understood. From her perspective, this is support. The minute he tries to fix the problem, she doesn't feel supported. But if he doesn't do anything about it, he doesn't feel he's supporting her. When a man solves a problem or has a solution, he builds testosterone. That's how he lowers his stress. You can see the dilemma.

I used to take my wife's complaints about anything and

everything personally. If we went to a nice restaurant and she said she didn't like the soup, I'd take it personally, as if she were insulting my ability to pick a nice place. It wasn't until I became a Mars Venus coach that I learned, when she complains, she's not taking a jab at me; she's just talking to me. She's bonding with me. I had never looked at it that way before.

When we learn how to love more authentically, to understand with more empathy, to work with one another better, and to embrace our differences, the world becomes a better place. That's John Gray's objective, and we, as Mars Venus coaches, have been personally trained by him to go out into the world and teach others how to effectively navigate their relationships, both personal and professional. As he discovered, he's only one guy, and he can't do it alone. Now we have hundreds of coaches in 40-some countries who are coaching and changing lives with the Mars Venus philosophy.

HOW CAN WE NOT USE GENDER INTELLIGENCE?

I'm an animal person. I've trained many different types of animals on my ranch. When training a dog, say you point to a tree, the dog will automatically look where your finger is pointing. The dog understands that you're pointing to the tree. If you do that to a cat, however, the cat will look at the end of your finger. They don't make that connection past your finger; they just think your finger is moving. This is clear evidence that their brains work differently. It's the same with men and women. How can you coach a man the same way you coach a woman? You can't.

To be a good coach or run a successful business, gender intelligence is a must. John Gray's methodologies have changed my way of thinking. When I first started out, it never occurred to me that coaching should be gender-specific. Now, after seeing the positive, transformative effects that gender intelligence and the Mars Venus coaching approach has on people, I've become a more empathetic coach, husband, father, and friend.

> Just as a man is fulfilled through working out
> the intricate details of solving a problem,
> a woman is fulfilled through talking
> about the dynamic of her problems.
>
> **DR. JOHN GRAY**

ENDNOTES

1 CDC. 2025. "Marriage and Divorce." Accessed September 5, 2025. https://www.cdc.gov/nchs/fastats/marriage-divorce.htm; Hayes, Jeff. 2008. "Workplace Conflict and How Businesses Can Harness It to Thrive." *CPP*. Accessed September 5, 2025. https://img.en25.com/Web/CPP/Conflict_report.pdf.

2 Wang, Jiongjiong, Marc Korczykowski, Hengyi Rao, Yong Fan, John Pluta, Ruben C. Gur, Bruce S. McEwen, and John A. Detre. 2007. "Gender Difference in Neural Response to Psychological Stress." *Social Cognitive and Affective Neuroscience* 2, no. 3 (September): 227–239. doi.org/10.1093/scan/nsm018; Taylor, S. E., L. C. Klein, B. P. Lewis, T. L. Gruenewald, R. A. Gurung, and J. A. Updegraff. 2000. "Biobehavioral Responses to Stress in Females: Tend-and-Befriend, Not Fight-or-Flight." *Psychological Review* 107, no. 3 (July): 411–429, doi.org/10.1037/0033-295x.107.3.411.

3 Peacock, Kimberly, Karen Carlson, and Kari M. Ketvertis. 2023. "Menopause." *StatPearls* (December). https://www.ncbi.nlm.nih.gov/books/NBK507826/.

4 Liang, Gengfan, Audrey Siew Foong Kow, Rohana Yusof, Chau Ling Tham, Yu-Cheng Ho, and Ming Tatt Lee. 2024. "Menopause-Associated Depression: Impact of Oxidative Stress and Neuroinflammation on the Central Nervous System-A Review." *Biomedicines* 12, no. 1 (January): 184. doi.org/10.3390/biomedicines12010184.

5 Born, Leslie, Gideon Koren, Elizabeth Lin, and Meir Steiner. 2008. "A New, Female-Specific Irritability Rating Scale." *Journal of Psychiatry & Neuroscience* 33, no. 4 (July): 344–354. https://pmc.ncbi.nlm.nih.gov/articles/PMC2440789; Healthdirect Australia. 2023. "Perimenopause." Accessed September 3, 2025. https://www.healthdirect.gov.au/perimenopause.

6 Sliwinski, Jim R., Aimee K. Johnson, and Gary R. Elkins. 2014. "Memory Decline in Peri- and Post-Menopausal Women: The Potential of Mind-Body Medicine to Improve Cognitive Performance." *Integrative Medicine Insights* 9 (August): 17–23. doi.org/10.4137/IMI.S15682.

7 Talesnik, Dana. 2019. "Eurich Explores Why Self-Awareness Matters." *NIH Record*. Accessed July 16, 2025. https://nihrecord.nih.gov/2019/06/28/eurich-explores-why-self-awareness-matters.

8 Roser, Max, Cameron Appel, and Hannah Ritchie. 2024. "Human Height." *Our World in Data*. Accessed May 1, 2025. https://ourworldindata.org/human-height.

9 Guiness World Records. n.d. "Rumeysa Gelgi: The Tallest Woman." Accessed May 1, 2025. https://www.guinnessworldrecords.com/records/hall-of-fame/rumeysa-gelgi-the-tallest-woman-living.

10 Gray, John. 1993. *What You Feel, You Can Heal: A Guide for Enriching Relationships*. John Gray's Mars Venus LLC.

11 Gray, John. 1993. *What You Feel, You Can Heal: A Guide for Enriching Relationships*. John Gray's Mars Venus LLC.

12 Cost, Katherine T., Piyumi Mudiyanselage, Eva Unternaehrer, Daphne J. Korczak, Jennifer Crosbie, Evdokia Anagnastou, Suneeta Monga, Elizabeth Kelley, Russell Schachar, Jonathon Maguire, Paul Arnold, Christie L. Burton, Stelios Georgiades, Rob Nicolson, Catherine S. Birken, and Alice Charach. 2023. "The Role of Parenting Practices in Parent and Child Mental Health Over Time." *BJPsych Open* 9, no. 5 (August): doi.org/10.1192/bjo.2023.529.

13 Collins, Lois M. 2016. "What 'Shared Parenting' Is and How It Can Affect Kids After Divorce." *Deseret News*, February 5. https://www.deseret.com/2016/2/5/20581666/what-shared-parenting-is-and-how-it-can-affect-kids-after-divorce/.

14 Farrelly, Daniel and Daniel Nettle. 2007. "Marriage Affects Competitive Performance in Male Tennis Players." *Journal of Evolutionary Psychology* 5 (March): 141–148. doi.org/10.1556/JEP.2007.1004.

15 Freud, Sigmund. 1921. *Group Psychology and the Analysis of the Ego*. Vienna: Internationaler Psychoanalytischer Verlag.

16 Acevedo, Bianca P., Arthur Aron, Helen E. Fisher, and Lucy L. Brown. 2012. "Neural Correlates of Long-Term Intense Romantic Love." *Social Cognitive and Affective Neuroscience* 7, no. 2 (January): 145–159. doi.org/10.1093/scan/nsq092.

17 Barry, Kristen, Kate Den Houter, and Karen Guggenheim. 2024. "More Than a Program: A Culture of Women's Well-being at Work." *Gallup*, December 4. https://www.gallup.com/workplace/653843/program-culture-women-well-being-work.aspx?.

18 Florida State University. 2012. "In Sickness and in Health: Importance of Supportive Spouses in Coping with Work-Related Stress." *ScienceDaily*, February 16. www.sciencedaily.com/releases/2012/02/120216165458.htm.

19 Swann, Teal. 2024. "The Truth About Parental Alienation - Teal Swan." April 13. Educational video, 25:20. https://youtu.be/tecX9fTMmi8.

20 Ellington, Laurie. 2024. "The Neuroscience of Coaching." *Global Wellness Institute*, May 1. https://globalwellnessinstitute.org/global-wellness-institute-blog/2024/05/01/the-neuroscience-of-coaching/.

21 Duckworth, Angela Lee. 2013. "Grit: The Power of Passion and Perseverance | Angela Lee Duckworth | TED." TED. May 10. TED talk, 6:12. https://youtu.be/H14bBuluwB8.

22 Prudente, Tiago Paiva, Eleazar Mezaiko, Erika Aparecida Silveira, and Tulio Eduardo Nogueira. 2024. "Effect of Dancing Interventions on Depression and Anxiety Symptoms in Older Adults: A Systematic Review and Meta-Analysis." *Behavioral Sciences* 14, no. 1 (January). doi.org/10.3390/bs14010043.

23 Salihu, Dauda, Rick Yiu Cho Kwan, and Eliza Mi Ling Wong. 2021. "The Effect of Dancing Interventions on Depression Symptoms, Anxiety, and Stress in Adults Without Musculoskeletal Disorders: An Integrative Review and Meta-Analysis." *Complementary Therapies in Clinical Practice* 45 (November). doi.org/10.1016/j.ctcp.2021.101467.

24 Fong Yan, Alycia, Leslie L. Nicholson, Rachel E. Ward, Claire E. Hiller, Kathryn Dovey, Helen M. Parker, Lee-Fay Low, Gene Moyle, and Cliffton Chan. 2024. "The Effectiveness of Dance Interventions on Psychological and Cognitive Health Outcomes Compared with Other Forms of Physical Activity: A Systematic Review with Meta-Analysis." *Sports Med* 54 (January): 1179–1205. doi.org/10.1007/s40279-023-01990-2.

25 Feireisen, Céline. 2024. "Le Leadership Féminin Est-il si Différent du Masculin?" *Le Devoir*, March 2. https://www.ledevoir.com/societe/808142/leadership-feminin-est-il-si-different-masculin.

26 Sapienza, Paola, Luigi Zingales, and Dario Maestripieri. 2009. "Gender Differences in Financial Risk Aversion and Career Choices Are Affected by Testosterone." *Proceedings of the National Academy of Sciences of the United States of America* 106, no. 36 (August): 15268–15273. doi.org/10.1073/pnas.0907352106.

27 Nivez, Catherine. 2018. "Finance: Le Goût Du Risque, Une Question De Testostérone?" *Forbes,* August 21. https://www.forbes.fr/finance/finance-le-gout-du-risque-une-question-de-testosterone/.

28 Christov-Moore, Leonardo, Elizabeth A. Simpson, Gino Coudé, Kristina Grigaityte, Marco Iacoboni, and Pier Francesco Ferrari. 2014. "Empathy: Gender Effects in Brain and Behavior." *Neuroscience and Biobehavioral Reviews* 46 (November): 604–627. doi.org/10.1016/j.neubiorev.2014.09.001.

29 Cohen Raphael H. 2021. "Pourquoi le Cerveau des Femmes ne les Prédispose pas à Réussir en Entreprise." *Harvard Business Review,* April 1. https://www.hbrfrance.fr/chroniques-experts/2021/03/33729-pourquoi-le-cerveau-des-femmes-ne-les-predispose-pas-a-reussir-en-entreprise/.

30 Ministry of Health and Social Services. 2018. "Health and Well-Being Statistics by Sex - All Quebec." *Government of Quebec*. Accessed April 30, 2025. https://www.msss.gouv.qc.ca/professionnels/statistiques-donnees-sante-bien-etre/statistiques-de-sante-et-de-bien-etre-selon-le-sexe-volet-national/acces-a-un-medecin-regulier/.

31 Statistics Canada. 2003. "Table 2.1.19 Frequency of doctor visits in the last 12 months, by age group and sex, 2003." Accessed April 30, 2025. https://www150.statcan.gc.ca/n1/pub/89-519-x/2006001/t/4122026-fra.htm.

32 Cucchi, Maud. 2022. "La Santé des Femmes, une Autre Source D'inégalités." *CBC Radio-Canada,* March 8. https://ici.radio-canada.ca/nouvelle/1864448/inegalite-femmes-sante-medecine-sexisme-recherche-ontario.

33 Ingalhalikar, Madhura, Alex Smith, Drew Parker, Theodore D. Satterthwaite, Mark A. Elliott, Kosha Ruparel, Hakon Hakonarson, Raquel E. Gur, and Ragini Verma. 2014. "Sex Differences in the Structural Connectome of the Human Brain." *Proceedings of the National Academy of Sciences of the United States of America* 111, no. 2 (December): 823–828. doi.org/10.1073/pnas.1316909110.

www.ingramcontent.com/pod-product-compliance
Lightning Source LLC
Chambersburg PA
CBHW062032290426
44109CB00026B/2603